6-1-79

WRITERS AND POLITICS
IN MODERN ITALY

# Writers and Politics
## in Modern Italy

John A. Gatt-Rutter

HOLMES & MEIER PUBLISHERS, INC.
NEW YORK

ar 030

79 8749 3

*Writers and Politics in Modern Italy* is one of a series of books under the general editorship of Professor John Flower. The other books in the series are as follows:

*Writers and Politics in Modern Britain* (J. A. Morris)
*Writers and Politics in Modern Germany* (C. E. Williams)
*Writers and Politics in Modern France* (J. E. Flower)
*Writers and Politics in Modern Scandinavia* (Janet Mawby)
*Writers and Politics in Modern Spain* (J. Butt)
*Writers and Politics in Modern Russia* (M. A. Nicholson)

First published in the United States of America 1978 by
Holmes & Meier Publishers, Inc.
30 Irving Place, New York, N.Y. 10003

**Library of Congress Cataloging in Publication Data**

Gatt-Rutter, J.A.
    Writers and politics in modern Italy.
    Bibliography: p.
    1. Italian literature — 20th century — History and criticism.
    2. Italy — Politics and government — 1945. 3. Politics in literature.
    I. Title.
    PQ4088.G3      850'.9'00914      78-188829

    ISBN 0-8419-0416-2

Printed in Great Britain.

# Foreword

The term 'political literature' like 'committed literature' with which it is frequently associated has become an accepted part of the language of literary history. Yet however convenient, it is, on examination, surprisingly imprecise and misleading. The whole area of the interaction between politics and literature is a vast and complex one which has yet, especially on a European scale, to be fully and comprehensively charted. Certainly invaluable contributions do already exist: Jean-Paul Sartre's *Qu'est-ce que la littérature?* (1947), George Woodcock's *The Writer and Politics* (1948), Jürgen Rühle's *Literatur und Revolution* (1960), Irving Howe's *Politics and the Novel* (1961), John Mander's *The Writer and Commitment* (1961) for example. There are too, as the bibliographical information contained in the individual essays in this series will reveal, a number of equally important books which deal with the issue in purely national terms. With few exceptions, however, these, like many of the more general studies, suffer from the same defects resulting in the main from a failure to distinguish adequately between 'political literature' and what might be termed 'social literature', and from an incomplete assessment of changes both in political climates and in the writer's relationship to society as a whole. Yet, even when the area of investigation and terminology has been more carefully ascertained, we often find that these books are principally concerned either with an examination of the political ideas *per se* contained in various works of literature, or with an assessment of the ways in which parties and movements have controlled and used to best advantage writers and intellectuals who claim political allegiance. More recently Roland Barthes in *Le Degré Zéro de l'écriture* (1967), George Steiner in *Language and Silence* (1967) and David Caute in *The Illusion* (1971) have suggested a wider perspective, outlining some of the problems of style and form which an imaginative writer has to face when he offers his pen to a political (or social) cause. On the whole, however, it is fair to say that the majority of critics have concentrated more on *what* ideas are expressed than on *how* they have been. In addition therefore to attempting to define the concept of political literature more precisely and to exploring such issues as the suitability of imaginative literature as a vehicle for political ideas or the effect such literature can have on the public, for example, one of the principal concerns of these essays is to attempt to examine ways in which an author's political sympathy or affiliation can be seen to affect or even dictate the way in which he writes. In some countries – in Russia, France or Spain, for example – direct influence of this kind is more apparent than in others. Elsewhere, notably in Britain, where political directives concerning art and literature have not been the rule, the problem is in some ways more difficult to assess. Indeed national variation of this kind is one of the principal contributory factors to the complex nature of the whole question. Thus while the subject is best illustrated and examined in the literature of France and Germany during the interwar years, it is after the Second World War that it fully emerges in the works of Italian and Scandinavian writers. Furthermore literary experiment seen and approved in some countries as an expression of a progressive, even revolutionary, political position is considered in others to be characteristic of subversion and decadence.

Given such problems as these and given too the amount of space available, the seven essays in these two volumes can do little more than hope to encourage a new approach to political literature. While free to explore the subject in the way they believe to be most useful within the context of the literary history of their particular countries, contributors have been encouraged to balance general comment with examination of specific examples. Inevitably therefore the essays appear arbitrarily selective. But like the literature which they choose to examine it is hoped that they will be judged not only for what they contain as for the ways in which they deal with it.

## General Bibliography

The following are a selection of those books which discuss some of the general problems associated with this subject. Suggestions for further reading are contained in the notes to individual essays.

BARTHES, Roland, *Le Degré Zéro de l'écriture*, Editions du Seuil, Paris, 1953 (Translated: *Writing Degree Zero*, Cape, London, 1967.)
CAUTE, David, *The Illusion: An Essay on Politics, Theatre and the Novel*, Deutsch, London, 1971.

CROSSMAN, Richard, *The God that Failed: Six Studies in Communism*, Hamish Hamilton, London, 1950.

HOWE, Irving, *Politics and the Novel*, Horizon Press, New York, 1955.

MANDER, John, *The Writer and Commitment*, Secker & Warburg, London, 1961.

MUIR, Edwin, *Essays on Literature and Society*, Hogarth Press, London, 1965.

PANICHAS, George, A. *(ed.)*, *The Politics of Twentieth-Century Novelists*, Crowell, New York, 1974.

RÜHLE, Jürgen, *Literatur und Revolution*, Kipenheuer & Witz, 1960. (Translated: *Literature and Revolution*, Pall Mall, London, 1969.)

SARTRE, Jean-Paul, *Qu'est-ce que la littérature?*, Gallimard, Paris, 1948. (Translated: *What is Literature?*, Methuen, London, 1951.)

STEINER, George, *Language and Silence: Essays and Notes, 1958-66*, Faber, London, 1967.

TROTSKY, Leon, *Literature and Revolution*, University of Michigan Press, Ann Arbor, 1960.

WINEGARTEN, Renée, *Writers and Revolution: the fatal lure of action*, Franklin Watts, New York, 1974.

WOODCOCK, George, *The Writer and Politics*, The Porcupine Press, London, 1948.

John Flower

And thou art here, for thou art less than they.

Keats

*(The Fall of Hyperion)*

Oh, che profumo di gigli e giornali di sinistra!

P. P. Pasolini

*(Affabulazione)*

for Thérèse

*Contents*

Introduction
The Literature of Politics and the
Politics of Literature in Italy

# Acknowledgments

My thanks are due to Ms Margaret Jarvis for much hard work in preparing the text and to Ms Jane Humphreys for helpful advice and information on political ideas and developments, as well as reading and commenting on the text throughout. I also wish to thank Dr J. R. Woodhouse for generously making available much material on and by Calvino; Professor John Saville, for making available material on rural society in Italy; Dr Mina J. Moore-Rinvolucri for her kind advice on Guareschi; Professor B. Moloney, Dr F. J. Hoyles, Mr H. F. Woodhouse, Mr J. C. Barnes and Mr P. J. Bromley for patiently reading and commenting on my text. The staff of the Brynmor Jones Library at the University of Hull have been of great service, and Professor P. M. Brown formerly of the Department of Italian at the University of Hull has done much to facilitate the writing of this essay. I am deeply grateful to Professor J. E. Flower, General Editor of this symposium, for his friendly and patient support and advice at every stage of work. Finally, I would like to thank Lily Arrigo, of Lija, Malta, for the warm hospitality extended by herself and Tancred, whom we bitterly mourn, without which this essay would not have been completed.

The writing of this book was completed in 1974, and since then only minor details have been amended or added. It has not been possible to take full account of work on the writers of the period under study which has appeared since 1974.

# Introduction

# The Literature of Politics and the Politics of Literature in Italy

The literature of a nation that has produced the *Divina Commedia* need not fear soiling its hands with politics – that is, the practical business of ordering human affairs. The *Divina Commedia* was clearly written as Dante's last and mightiest attempt – desperate and, as it proved, futile – to change the whole course of European history. Up to 1301, Dante had kept literature and politics separate: on the one hand, his poetry in the *dolce stil novo* and his *Vita nuova*; on the other, his active participation in the Guelf victory at Campaldino and in the government of the city-state of Florence. After his exile and exclusion from active politics, writing and political concern grow together, and each grows deeper and broader. The *Convivio* and *De Monarchia* give Dante's theoretical answer to the breakdown of feudal Christendom; his letters to the Florentine government, to the Italian city-states and to the Emperor Henry VII are his last direct attempt to have this solution realised. After Henry's failure, Dante tries to win the conscience of his fellow Italians by presenting to them, in the homely and vigorous Italian of the *Commedia*, a Christian statement of the human condition in all its aspects and under the twofold perspective of universal and contemporary history (or politics). His poetic masterpiece, however, was an anachronism and a failure at the level of practical politics.

The pen (or even the typewriter) is in fact rarely mightier than the florin (or the dollar). Perhaps it is this logic in the nature of things that explains why the Petrarchan has tended to prevail over the Dantesque current in the literature of Italy. 'Beauty' flowers more readily in the gardens of Power than on the battlefields where Power is challenged. Petrarch, indeed, enthusiastically hailed Cola di Rienzo's attempt to revive the ancient Roman Republic and wrote some lively poems encouraging the Italian princes to unite the country or launch a

3

crusade against the Infidel and vituperating Papal corruption. But this is the small change of political literature, not part of an all-embracing perspective of human experience. Petrarch's real contribution is to the politics of literature rather than the literature of politics: as the first 'man of letters', he fathered the illusion of the autonomy of culture from politics. Illusion is fathered from illusion: for the autonomy of culture rests, in Petrarch, on the notion of the self as an autonomous universe to whose dramatic inner conflicts are subordinated the conflicting external realities of the prevailing social values – courtly Love and Christianity. These two forces of the social world exist in Petrarch's poetry only as poetic projections of the conscious self. All external values or realities can therefore be poeticised, emptied of their value or reality, in the same way as the individual, in his absolute autonomy, is illusorily emptied of his social, psychological and physical reality to become his own aesthetic abstraction. All this, which is, in Petrarch, only half conscious, only half intentional, becomes the very essence of the main stream of the Italian literary tradition right up to the Second World War and represents the padded cell out of which most Italian writers since the war have desperately been trying to escape, while some, like Montale or Cassola, have proudly and stubbornly (and not without dialectical subtlety) barricaded themselves inside it.

Petrarch's own experience illustrates how ambiguous is the individual's autonomy, which brings dramatic intensity to his poetry precisely because, from the first, it was highly problematical. For there is no doubt that, to the self, the only reality is the consciousness of the self (as at once subject and object). This is the irreducible foundation of the mental liberty of the individual. Yet that consciousness can be defined, expressed, experienced only dialectically, through what is external to itself. Petrarch, thinking antithetically rather than dialectically, must forever find his supposed autonomy imprisoned: within a prescribed Christianity, within unfulfilled desires, within his own style and within language itself. His successors, six hundred years later, strongly neo-Petrarchan poets such as Ungaretti and Quasimodo, saw the trap.* Ungaretti: 'Ho fatto a pezzi cuore e mente / per cadere in servitù di parole?' ['Have I cut heart and mind to pieces / to fall into the bondage of words?']; Quasimodo: 'Ma se ti prendo, ecco: / parola tu pure mi sei e tristezza.' ['But if I seize

---

*Following quotes respectively in 'La pietà' from Il Sentimento del Tempo (1933) and 'Parola', from Oboe sommerso (1932).

you, see: / you too are but a word, and sorrow.'] Thus they express the predicament of the traditional 'man of letters' or the latter-day 'intellectual' whose trade is words. For if Petrarch was the first important writer to gain some real independence from both the feudal rulers and the Church (combining the poetic fantasy of the one culture with the intellectual seriousness of the other) and thus encroach on the Church's monopoly of moral thought and intellectual values, he also virtually inaugurated a new meritocratic *class* of writers, whose pens were for hire. This brought with it two dangers, which have been with us ever since. One is that writers and their culture might be sealed off hermetically within their own 'class', with little interest in, contact with, or influence on, a predominantly Philistine or culture-starved society: 'society' and 'culture' lose touch with one another. The other danger is that the writer can only further the interests of those who pay him, which may mean, willy-nilly, reinforcing existing power-relationships or class-relationships within society. These are dilemmas, as we shall see, which recent Italian writers have tried hard, or claimed to try hard, to escape, but with a degree of success far from satisfactory to themselves.

Petrarch's example shows that literature cannot escape from politics, least of all when it tries to do so. Political implications in literature go beyond the author's conscious intentions or the reader's conscious response. Jane Austen's *Emma* and R. L. Stevenson's *Treasure Island* are objectively assertions of the values and privileges of the English gentry and of the rightness of the established order. (They may obviously be a lot more besides.) On the part of the authors, this must be at least partly conscious; to the reader (especially the ten-year-old reading *Treasure Island*), the fact may be much less apparent. So Ariosto's *Orlando furioso* can be seen as a celebration of the new court aristocracy, with its new code of honour, its mania for duelling and its light-hearted amorousness.

We can go further. The political content of a literary work may actually be opposed to the author's intentions. Dante's universe in the *Divina Commedia* is, in every sense but one, theocentric. The poet's thesis is that human nature can fulfil itself only through God and through a divinely-ordained social order. But despite the supreme poetry of Dante's vision of God in the final canto, it is men and women, not the Divine Trinity, who fill the poem. And what is more, Dante puts the most fascinating people in Hell and gives them most of his best lines. So that – particularly since the dawning of romanticism

– it is the human rather than the divine that has drawn readers to the *Commedia*, and a scholar of Auerbach's stature has entitled his study *Dante – Poet of the Secular World*. The *Paradiso* itself is the vision of a joyous *human* community in which the sight of the Divine Essence acts to unite all individuals together in a choreographic unanimity of music and light, 'il riso dell'universo'. The complications for us are therefore considerable and suggest, I think, that the political dimension of a work of literature is no mere matter of promoting the 'ideology' of a party – Catholic or Communist, reactionary, conservative, liberal, reformist or revolutionary; or of conveying class attitudes; or of favouring or opposing any particular movement or institution – parliamentary democracy or dictatorship, women's rights or racial purity, economic inequality or environmental pollution: though any of these might be involved. Politics involves a total view of humanity, of the relation between human beings and the world, themselves and one another. This is why politics is inseparable from literary endeavour: indeed, it provides a means of objectively evaluating artistic achievement. Literary evaluation cannot escape from being simultaneously political evaluation. We can determine whether the literary work is merely and solely an instrument for furthering an immediate and limited political design by examining how the literary work presents people, and how interestingly it does so, and by studying the author's own relation to his public and enquiring whether he writes for or to a limited section of society.

This last criterion calls for amplification. Literary culture today is still restricted to a pitifully small proportion of the population, even in countries where at least elementary literacy is supposed to be universal. In Italy, for instance, even after the 'paperback revolution', only one twentieth-century literary work (Lampedusa's *Il gattopardo*) has topped a million copies sold, and only the barest handful of books have approached that figure. The cinema, television and radio are the mediums through which literature has the best chance of reaching most people. *Fumetti* – film-strip comics – are by far the most popular form of 'reading' in Italy today. All these mediums imply central control and diffusion (the broadcasting station or the publishing corporation) and a passive recipient (viewer, listener or reader). This is the structure of modern mass-communications. Even where genuine audience participation takes place, in the form of 'phone-in programmes or open forums and suchlike, the initiative remains inevitably and overwhelmingly with those who control the medium.

Literature is not quite a typical case. True, the writer has a God-like omnipotence over the blank page before him, as the publisher might have over the writer. But the reader of books, though rarer than the television viewer, has more opportunity to choose between different authors or books than the viewer between programmes or films. And likewise, the writer has more publishers to choose from than programme directors or film-makers. The main hazards for the writer thus remain the narrowness of his readership and the solitude both of the act of writing and of the act of reading. This solitude is a perpetual temptation to solipsism and the Petrarchan fallacy, especially so when, in many 'advanced' countries, the culture industry tends more and more to become a closed and self-contained cycle in which the product – books, in our case – is consumed within the industry itself, which thus takes on some of the characteristics of a Church. Publishing, educational and academic establishments, and writers, all sustain each other on a net inflow of funds from the public purse.

# Chapter One

# People and Politics in post-war Italy

Politically, the Italy of today is fundamentally the Italy which emerged from the collapse of Fascism in 1943. The monarchy, irreparably compromised, was voted out, narrowly, in 1946, but the presence of British and American forces ensured that liberation was not accompanied by any other radical change. Returning from exile in Moscow in 1944, the Italian Communist leader, Togliatti, announced that Italy must complete its bourgeois revolution before it could have a proletarian revolution and that therefore his party would work with others – even, if necessary, with the monarchy and the Church – in a broad democratic government. Theory thus adapted itself to military fact.

In the industrial north of Italy, still occupied until 1945 by the Germans who propped up a puppet Fascist regime under Mussolini, opposition to the Nazis and Fascists by workers, citizens and the armed partisan bands of the Resistance, organised in thousands of Comitati di Liberazione Nazionale in almost every town and factory, reached a scale of magnitude unmatched anywhere else in German-occupied Europe. Anti-Fascists of all political persuasions or of none joined in the Italian Resistance, and it is hard to exaggerate the atmosphere generated as huge masses of people took the political initiative directly into their own hands. The Communists were by far the most numerous (including such writers as Vittorini, Carlo Levi, Pratolini and Calvino) and the best organised, while the Partito d'Azione, which wanted a radical democratic revolution without class warfare, had a strong following among intellectuals, as well as among the partisans, and hoped that the CLN would provide the new structure of popular democracy that was to emerge in Italy from the war. The millions of Communist followers in the CLN, for their part, expected that a social revolution and a workers' state would follow naturally from the liberation. But none of the major political forces in Italy welcomed the prospect of power being wielded directly by the people. The Communist leadership were opposed to such 'left-wing extremism', as Lenin had called it, and were wedded to the idea of the leading role of the Party – that is, themselves. For their part, the British and the Americans, the Church and the Christian Democrats, big business and the Liberal party, the monarchy, the southern landowners and the monarchist party, all combined to preserve the country's traditional power-structure in all essentials. Parri's CLN government, receiving total support only from the Partito d'Azione and some Socialists and Republicans, ruled Italy for only five brief months in 1945.

The able Christian Democrat leader, De Gasperi, rapidly effected a polarisation of Italian politics on anti-Communist lines, and, though the Communists persistently sought an anti-Fascist coalition with the Christian Democrats and other parties (as they are still doing today), both the Communists and the Socialists were manoeuvred out of the government in May 1947. Ever since then the Christian Democrats have been continually in office, and the influence of the Vatican has flourished. However, the Christian Democrats have not had an absolute majority since 1953, and the delicate political equilibrium has produced a curious combination of immobility and instability, with an average of one change of government every year. The most pressing reforms – the very provisions of the Republic's 1947 Constitution – have been extraordinarily difficult, if not impossible, to implement. Even the biggest single achievement of Italian government since the war has been a half-measure. This is the Cassa del Mezzogiorno, which has started to reverse the age-old impoverishment of the South. This impoverishment had actually been accelerating since the Unification. The Cassa has devoted large funds to land reclamation, road-building, technical assistance (especially for agriculture) and business incentives, and, from 1960 onwards, it has created centres of heavy industry. Also, under pressure from the peasants, who were seizing land for themselves in 1950, and in fear of the spread of Communist influence among them, there was some redistribution of the land. Most of these measures were inadequate, paternalistic, divisive, and usually out of touch with the people's real social character and needs, and millions of southerners have had to seek work in the alien, industrial North or in foreign lands. And among those who remain, unemployment and under-employment are still massive problems.

This parallels the case of Italy as a whole. The country has enjoyed, rather briefly, an economic miracle and has adopted the policies of

9

consumer economics and improving welfare provisions. Yet emigration is still tacitly encouraged as the answer to unemployment, in default of increased internal investment, so that many Italian workers produce wealth for other countries instead of in their own homeland and have to undergo new kinds of social stress. At the same time, agriculture has been neglected, so that some land has gone out of cultivation and the rural way of life is fast disintegrating, while full employment is still a distant dream.

The Christian Democrats and their political allies brought Italy into the Western military camp by signing the NATO agreement in 1949, and they also made the country a founder-member of the European Economic Community. The Communists and Socialists bitterly attacked these alignments in foreign policy but restrained the wage demands of their own trade union members, still hoping for a share in government. The Socialists did indeed join in Centre-Left coalitions from 1963, but the Communists' search for respectability resulted in a decline of the Party's direct influence over the trade unions in the North and the peasant masses in the South and a drop in membership: though, paradoxically, their voting strength has climbed steadily from one-fifth to well over a third of the electorate.

The Church has moved from a policy of direct and vigorous influence on events to a more discreet one. Though, in helping to frame Italy's 1947 Constitution, the Communists were extraordinarily accommodating and allowed the privileges which the Church had won from Mussolini in 1929 to stand, the Church was uncompromisingly hostile to Communism and, after the Christian Democrats' electoral victory in 1948, excommunicated all Communist voters. This policy was eventually reversed by Pope John XXIII (1958-63), who reciprocated the Soviet and Italian Communist policy of peaceful coexistence. But, more than anti-Communism or the absence of it, an important feature of the Church today is that, despite its reiterated condemnations of 'modern materialism' (which some may see as attempts to discourage wage-demands), the Holy See has become inextricably enmeshed in both the economic and the political machinery of advanced capitalism. Though it now no longer tries to establish a controlling interest in companies large or small, private, public or state-directed, its role as a grey eminence in both economics and politics has lessened its authority in people's minds. The Church used all its influence to repeal the divorce act in the 1974 referendum, but three voters out of five thought differently. Italy's breakneck transition since the war from a predominantly agrarian to an overwhelmingly urban society has also worked to break down traditional pieties. Yet there has been a religious resurgence of radical Catholics, with the cry 'La Chiesa siamo noi!' ['We are the Church!']

From the late 1960s, anticipating even the revolt of May 1968 in Paris, there has been a broad groundswell of discontent and dissent in Italy, no less strong in the growingly united trade union movement than in the antiquated universities and schools. Both students and workers have obtained limited improvements, though their official political and trade organisations have usually been rather reluctant to be led by their followers. At the same time, there have been several abortive conspiracies of a Fascist character to seize power by *coup d'état* or armed insurrection, with ample financial backing, and there have also been numerous bomb outrages and other acts of terrorism, which the authorities have been suspiciously slow, despite the evidence, to pin firmly on to various clandestine neo-Fascist organisations. In the last few years, impatience with the Catholic and the Communist establishments has resulted in considerable left-wing terrorism also.

## Towards the suicide of literature?

In striking contrast to writers in the English-speaking countries, Italian writers since the war have kept political issues at the forefront of their literary awareness and, in intention at least, have tried to contribute to the national renewal of their country by bringing literature closer to the people or by using literature to combat or demystify the power-structures of their country. Their twin initial inspirations were the Resistance movement and the posthumous works of Antonio Gramsci. There was thus a great spate of Resistance novels and other 'neo-realistic' works, many of them written by men or women without any professional literary training. This was accompanied, in poetry, by a reaction against the private musings and stylistic preciosity of the lyric poets of the pre-war 'hermetic' school and by a return to the poet's civic responsibilities. What gave an intellectual framework and direction to this whole movement within literature was the posthumous publication of the notebooks which Gramsci, the Italian Communist Party leader, wrote during his last years, spent in a Fascist prison.

11

Gramsci pointed out that Italy, more than most other European countries, had failed to develop a truly popular and national literature, just as it had failed to develop a strong and homogeneous national bourgeoisie and a modern social structure. It was still an extraordinarily oligarchic society: even modern industry had developed in the hands of a very small number of people. The most important task for progressive Italian writers was therefore to develop such a popular national literature.

This notion of Gramsci's, set out in tentative form as a guideline for a critical study of Italian culture which he meant to undertake, overlapped another of his working-notions: the idea of cultural hegemony. By this he meant the conventional ideology or values of a given society at a given time, the set of notions that are taken for granted by most people, such as feudal Christendom in the early Middle Ages or modern consumer capitalism or Marxist-Leninism. Gramsci believed that, within capitalist society, the intellectuals of the proletarian party might supplant the cultural hegemony of capitalism with a counter-culture and new values and thus speed up the transition to a classless society.

These two notions – that of a popular national culture and that of revolutionary cultural hegemony – did not really coincide, and neither of them now appears to have been practicable *in advance* of a revolution. Nevertheless, Gramsci's writings were read with enthusiasm by a great many of the writers who had shared the high hopes of the Resistance – partly, no doubt, because of the Communist thinker's bold and penetrating analysis of the centuries-old limitations of Italian literary culture, but also, one feels, because Gramsci's reflections offered them such a splendid justification for following, with a buoyant social conscience, their own chosen calling.

Armed with these notions, and with a strong sense of mission, the 'committed' writers quickly identified *neorealismo* as the ideal literary mode to transform the social conscience of the nation. The Italian Communist Party encouraged this attitude, officially adopted Gramsci's analysis of Italian society and his cultural policy, and presented itself as the natural home of progressive writers. *Neorealismo* also coincided well enough with Zhdanov's programme of 'socialist realism', which made its appearance in the USSR at about the same time. There were some early defections from the Communist Party, to be sure. Elio Vittorini, whose *Conversazione in Sicilia* in 1938 had sounded the literary death-knell of Fascism, was one of the first writers to join the Party, in 1941, and also one of the first to leave, in 1948. He did so after an exchange of open letters with Togliatti over the direction taken under Vittorini's editorship by the monthly *Il Politecnico* (1946-47), which stood for the new culture embodying the values of the Resistance. Vittorini's reasons for leaving were not strictly political. As he admitted in an article in *La Stampa* on 6 September 1951 (and in this he regards himself as typical of many intellectuals who joined the Party during the Resistance and then left it), his political notions were generic in the extreme. As Franco Fortini, the socialist intellectual, poet, critic and essayist, declared, 'Non fui io a impegnarmi nella politica attiva, fu la guerra che mi impegnò.* ['I did not commit *myself* to active politics: the war committed *me*.'] Rather, it was precisely over the autonomy of literature, his disinclination as a writer and an organiser of culture to subordinate individuality to the need to make the revolution, that Vittorini broke with the Party, arguing that literature could serve the revolution better if it were free than if it were subjected to political directives.

*Neorealismo* was challenged, then, even before it was properly under way, and by no less a person than Vittorini, who has acted both as leader and as a barometer, giving advance notice of changes in the literary atmosphere. Nevertheless, 'neo-realism' continued as the prevailing literary mode throughout the 1950s, until its limitations became generally apparent. There were three in particular: first, it was a literature about the people (often about a sentimentalised image of 'the people') but not for the people, as literature was and is essentially a middle-class consumer good; nor by the people, as it projected the values of authors who were middle-class at least by their education if not by their origins. Secondly, neo-realist literature dealt with the most archaic sectors of Italian society – the peasants, particularly those in the South, and the artisans of the traditional city centres – which industrial change was rapidly reducing to a few quaint or exotic survivals. Finally, though the neo-realist documentary approach should have entailed a salutary discipline and did produce some impressive results, it inclined to a naive and restricted notion of what constituted 'reality' which could easily degenerate into a parochial conventionalism. The neo-realistic writers thus appeared, on all these counts, to be indulging in nostalgic pieties or in what Vittorini called a new 'Arcadia', or again, to use Montale's phrase this

---

*In La generazione degli anni difficili, *ed. by* E. A. Albertoni, E. Antonini and R. Palmieri (1962), p. 147.

time, in one of the recurrent varieties of 'estetismo di sinistra': 'un realismo decadente che può produrre persino oggetti di lusso' ['aestheticism of the left': 'a decadent realism that can actually produce luxury goods'].

However, the real break with *neorealismo* did not come until 1956, the year when Khrushchev denounced the crimes of Stalin and then proceeded to crush the Hungarians' revolt against their own Stalinist system. Many left-wing intellectuals now rejected Communism as a power-structure in some ways more brutal, repressive and class-ridden than the capitalist system itself. Franco Fortini, in *Dieci inverni* (1957), describes their painful 'sfacelo ideologico' ['ideological collapse'] and dates from this time their equally painful political re-education, which, in many cases, led them to far more modern notions about the ways in which revolutionary intellectuals could combat the hegemony of world capitalism, whether draped in white, red or black.

Vittorini again led the way, in 1960, by facing the theme of 'industry and literature', in the journal *Il Menabò*. He warned against simply transferring the techniques of neo-realism from the village-square or the old *rione* or *quartiere* to the factory floor. He suggested that the best way for literature to deal with the new reality of industrial capitalism was to revise its own techniques to match the sophisticated techniques of modern industrial production. In particular, he argued that, as monopoly capitalism transforms all it touches, so literature should revolutionise its own productive system, which is language itself, so as to transform the conventional views of reality which language is used to construct and thus challenge the linguistic constructs which capitalism continually manufactures as the counterpart to, and validation of, its continuous manufacture and distribution of goods. Joyce and other 'modernist' writers were to become the presiding deities of the new literature.

As always, Vittorini – like virtually all Italian writers – thought ultimately, and even against his own conscious intentions, in terms of the autonomy of literature, with the result that he perpetuated the impotence of literature (except as an inert support to the capitalist process of production and consumption and the class culture that goes with it). Fascinated by modern industrial processes, Vittorini seems more interested in seeing their analogy in literature than in addressing literature to any other aim than gratuitous creation and, in effect, self-gratification for author and reader. Hence new sorts of 'estetismo di sinistra'.

14

The *avanguardia* and *neoavanguardia* and *sperimentali* took up his cue with considerable subversive, if purely verbal, vigour, which they turned at first mainly to poetry. They used various types of fragmented discourse, put together with deliberate randomness, drawing on different frames of reference and value-systems in strident incongruity, as a way of capturing the 'schizomorphism' of our modern world and thus countering it. Some have seen the systematic destruction of discourse and the suicide of literature as the only way in which literature can challenge the dominant value-system of our industrial consumer society – no doubt causing at least some discomfort to the publishing industry in search of new literary masterpieces.

In the novel, the suicide of literature took various forms: Sanguineti's belated surrealism; or, in Vassalli's *Tempo di Massacro* (1970), an arid parody of seventeenth-century pedantic discourse, fragmented in its syntax and even in its words, on the inadequacy of all forms of slaughter for the grand design of annihilating the human race; Balestrini's *Vogliamo tutto* (1971) relates, in the most uncompromising language of industrial agitation, as used by an immigrant Southern worker, the events of the 'hot autumn' of 1969 in the Fiat works.

McLuhan was probably more right about literature than about any other medium: that the medium *is* the message (and the massage). Writers have not radically changed the medium, and the massage is still literature. At best, it remains the conscience of the cultured class, at worst, its ornament.

# Chapter Two

# Nine Writers

The foregoing outline lays no claim to adequacy even as a brief summary of the literary history of the post-war period in Italy. Likewise, my selection of writers does not imply any absolute supremacy of these writers; in an essay which does not discuss Vittorini, Moravia or Gadda, that would be absurd. I have also omitted mention of Italy's many excellent women writers.

I have chosen, then, four writers who lived through their prime under Fascism but wrote their best work later, or in exile: Ugo Betti (1892-1953); Eugenio Montale (born in 1896); Ignazio Silone (an alias, now the legal name, of Secondo Tranquilli, born in 1900); and Cesare Pavese (1908-50). Giovanni Guareschi (1908-68) might be counted with these four or with two writers who entered adulthood on the fall of Fascism: Pier Paolo Pasolini (1922-75) and Italo Calvino (born in 1923). Finally, two lone novels: Giuseppe Tomasi di Lampedusa's *Il gattopardo*, which appeared and won immediate and unequalled celebrity in 1958, after the death of its elderly author (born in 1896); and *Luisa e il presidente*, written by a young author, Ugo Terruggi, which appeared in 1972 and has passed unnoticed.

Several of these authors – like many in Italy – have had other vocations besides literature: Betti was a judge; Montale wanted to sing in opera; Silone started as a full-time revolutionary; Guareschi did odd jobs and journalism; Pasolini is best known for his films; Calvino's first interest, and his university degree, were in science; Lampedusa, a somewhat impoverished aristocrat, turned to writing in his last years; Terruggi is a parliamentary recorder. Fame has looked askance at many of them. Besides Terruggi's case, *Il gattopardo* was turned down (by Vittorini) until after its author's death; Betti and Silone won slow and grudging recognition in Italy despite foreign acclaim, Betti receiving no mention in Manacorda's *Storia della letteratura italiana contemporanea* (which, however, omits the theatre completely) and Silone slightingly little. Guareschi is too popular to be mentionable in any literary history.

Politically, they are complex to characterise, as will appear from my accounts of them. Silone, Pavese, Pasolini and Calvino have all been in the Communist Party and left by various routes – suicide, in Pavese's case. Montale was a non-party anti-Fascist, has always been no less anti-Communist, and has lately supported Italy's most unequivocally capitalist party (the Liberals). Betti and Guareschi were more or less non-party quasi-Fascists, and Guareschi was editor of a periodical of the far Right (*Candido*). Lampedusa and Terruggi have kept their politics private, or literary.

## Ugo Betti: the whore as queen

Betti's concern with politics goes back at least as far as his degree thesis of 1914, *Il diritto e la rivoluzione* (included in *Scritti inediti*). This marries that somewhat incompatible couple, Marx and Nietzsche, and systematically subverts all established notions of law, justice, the state, religion, monogamy and the family, culture and liberty, seeing the pattern of history as the violent self-affirmation of the strongest and 'fittest'. Betti's own feast of violence in the Great War sickened him and changed his perspectives but never cancelled his youthful pre-war vision of the world: rather, he inverted his original values, positing, beneath all the 'noes', and beyond all reason, a redeeming 'yes' to our apparently pitiful human condition.*

But the 'noes' remain in Betti's drama and explain its potency. Their presence is so subversive, so unaccommodating to passively received truths, that his plays have been fiercely attacked from the Church side and by anti-clericals, by Fascists and anti-Fascists.

Some of his plays relate directly to current political issues. One of them, *Frana allo scalo Nord* (1931), combines this topical allusiveness with a basic political philosophy obliquely justifying the post-Concordat Fascist state which Italy had just become. Like all such philosophies, this one is rooted in the metaphysics of sin – not personal sin, but original sin, preceding all individual responsibility.

All Betti's plays are patient excavations into deeper and deeper layers of conscience to reveal a guilt that spares no one – and, beyond that, redemption. In *Frana* – as in several others – Betti draws on his

---

*See* Religione e teatro, *p. 32.*

experience as a judge to use the judicial enquiry as society's accepted means of establishing guilt and innocence, with stark ironic possibilities of contrasting society's justice with a higher ethic. To achieve this latter end, Betti uses devices which appear – though in considerably varied forms – in nearly all his plays. Symbolic suggestions crowd in on the realistic framework – witness, in this play, the blinding rain and the murderous landslide itself. Characters (including the investigating judge, Parsc) betray physical blemishes and private guilts and memories which are irrelevant, in a strict legal sense, to the case. The conventions of realism are most conspicuously flouted by the appearance of the mysterious 'Accusatore Generale', Goetz – embodiment of a higher justice – and of the dead victims of the landslide, whom he summons as witnesses.

The result is fascinating, if contrived (being both stagey and patently ideological). Each person implicated in the disaster begins by throwing the blame on to someone above him. The accusing finger eventually points to Kurz – in terms which clearly allude to the Duce of Fascism (Act III, Scene 1) – who is, for the sycophantic Jud, 'Una grande figura! Un vero padre! Un colosso!' ['A great figure! A real father! A colossus!'], but who is now eloquently accused of crushing the whole of society, living and dead, as in a wine-press (the images 'torchio', 'meccanismo', 'ingranaggio' are repeatedly used by Betti, both in his plays and in his essays, to characterise society).

Kurz now rounds on his accusers, accusing everybody else of being themselves the mechanism that devours him too along with them. Misery, fear and the self-seeking greed and rivalry which these engender drive the machine remorselessly on. No one in particular is guilty, yet all are guilty. Spurred on by Goetz, and by the universal need for judgment, Parsc can only pronounce for mercy – 'pietà'.

Betti thus justifies a political, social and economic system by its own weaknesses, metaphysically translated into the dualism of original sin and divine mercy. This is a concordat in which the Vatican and the priests are left suspiciously invisible. (In his own life, Betti sought a confessor only in his last months, after cancer had been diagnosed.) It is a model of Fascism which pretends that the Duce is as powerless as his victims, that the industrialists and landowners who put him in and the bureaucrats and opportunists from all walks of life who kept him in cannot be held particularly responsible for anything; that there was no political struggle but a unanimous, if unconscious, totalitarian urge; that Mussolini was no mere historical phenomenon but the twentieth-century expression of a timeless human situation. Betti's effortless universalism has been often, and usually uncritically, noted.

Overplaying the extent to which people (perhaps even napalm manufacturers?) are genuinely held by social and political structures and thus not individually responsible for what they do, Betti justifies the most murderous of structures and offers universal immoralism dressed up as universal moralism. *Frana* is dangerously close to a cynical use of the confessional.

Betti wrote no other play as deliberately political as *Frana*. *L'aiuola bruciata* (1952) bases its 'not by bread alone' message on the rather unreal presumption of a dictatorial affluent society. The sinister machinations of power in the play seem to be meant as a commentary on the Stalinist system. But the materialist consumerism which suffocates the citizens, allowing them no choice of alternatives or sublimations, and which accounts for Guido's suicide, seems closer to what is called the affluent West. Betti scores against the target of ruthless power-politics, but the soulless affluence is rather improbably, and only verbally, lugged in. As in *Frana*, Betti betrays a failure or a fear of concrete political and economic analysis and a failure in particular to understand the link between politics and economics. And as in *Frana*, the somewhat miraculous solution depends on a deliberately unreal characterisation: in this case, the uncorrupted Rosa. The real merits of the play lie in the dramatisation of the suppressed political conscience of the dead Guido's father, Giovanni.

*Corruzione nel palazzo della giustizia* (1945) is also disappointing politically. Again, Betti is more interested in Cust's diseased conscience than in the connections between judicial corruption and political power. He has reduced to a purely personal dimension a question relating to the political and social order.

*La regina e gli insorti* (1949), probably Betti's best play, evokes the atmosphere of the Resistance and early post-war Italy, when fear of red revolution was in the air and the future of the Italian monarchy was in the balance. In the play, revolution reeks of blood and is prosecuted mainly by fanatics or opportunists. However, the revolutionary leader Amos emerges as an impressive character and has a powerful speech (*Teatro completo*, pp. 1342-43): for him, the revolution turns out in the end to spring from a hitherto unconscious rage for destruction, for the total negation of an intolerable world. It is immediately upon this that the whore, Argia, makes her majestic exit from life as the charismatic queen so long hunted down by the rebels,

19

as the queen she had always felt herself to be. By contrast, the real queen has sunk into the most sordid degradation.

Who, then, is the real revolutionary – one may ask – when the despised Argia takes her stand before God unabashed, the most joyous of his creatures, not in voluntary self-sacrifice, but simply in the fearlessness of one faced with immediate death? Never did Betti more pointedly illustrate Marx's description of religion as 'the fantastic realisation of the human being inasmuch as the human being possesses no true reality . . . the sigh of the oppressed creature, the sentiment of a heartless world and the soul of soulless conditions'. In this tallest of his tall stories and melodramatic plots, Betti captures at its purest the pre-political, even pre-religious moment – what can fairly be called the existential moment of the self – when the self projects itself against death and against others. This reality of the self, keenly felt by Betti, obscurely pervades all his plays. It was present in the misery of each character in *Frana*. So closed was Betti's mind to concrete social analysis that he could present a person's real identity only in the extraordinary situation of *La regina e gli insorti*, and then only by having everybody mistake that person for someone at the opposite end of the social scale.

G. H. McWilliam has interestingly detected Betti's misinterpretation of the social 'message' of an earlier one of his own plays, *Una bella domenica di settembre*. Betti claims as a vindication of the family what is in fact an exposure of family life as a sham. There, too, a woman's dignity and her sexual liberty are involved: there, too, her role is mistaken – only this time the world keeps her trapped in her conventional role as a respectable mother when, in fact, she is engaged in an extra-matrimonial escapade.* Betti's deception, or self-deception, over this play points to his continual ambiguity with regard particularly to female sexuality. This is most evident in the ending of *Delitto all'isola delle capre* (1946): the attempted distinction between salvation and damnation fails; Agata, for all her 'bestial' sexuality and her murder of the Priapic male, Angelo, has simply realised her predetermined self. The turbulent Eros of Betti's plays always runs athwart the sanctity of marriage, which appears (even against the author's intentions) as an empty social fiction. If Eros is Sin, then we cannot help sinning. Yet, if we are not free not to sin, there can be no

---

*See G. H. McWilliam, 'The Minor Plays of Ugo Betti', in Italian Studies, XX (1965), pp. 78-107, esp. pp. 89-94.

sin. Plays such as *Delitto* and *Acque turbate* dramatise this paradox and attempt to resolve it: like Argia, the other protagonists, Agata and Giacomo, are simultaneously *in* sin and *above* it. They can 'stand up' to God.

In this field, where politics touches on what is most intimate in a person's life – love and sexuality – Betti is again, in effect, defending institutions – a rigorous monogamy and all its attendant taboos – while showing that human behaviour cannot be contained within them: the logic of the brothel or of Betti's own Goat Island. As long as human nature is regarded as sinful, divine authority remains secure. In all Betti's plays, this divine authority is internalised as the content of the individual conscience or externalised in symbolic personages such as Goetz or the Alto Revisore and is sanctified in his later plays by the sacrifice of inexplicably sinless nurses. Never does it take a concrete social form. In actual modern society, authority (divine or otherwise) takes on more corporeal and human forms and extremely tenacious structures and, all over our globe, claims real 'sinful' human beings as its sacrificial victims. Betti's *coscienza* brazenly begs the question of its own origin, which is the same as the question of authority in society, and this is his great political evasion. Yet few dramatists have equalled the force with which he presents the tensions within the old Catholic view as it faces the modern world.

## Manichee and hierophant: Montale's negative epiphany

Montale's *Satura* (1971) contains the poem 'Nel silenzio' (p. 153). This opens with the line 'Oggi è sciopero generale'. ['Today there's a general strike.'] and goes on for another eleven lines, each ending with a full stop, describing the incidental effects of the strike and irregularly marked by the deliberately banal rhyme in *-ale*. Then follows the abrupt switch of the poem's conclusion:

> Tu stai sotto una lapide. Risvegliarti non vale
> perché sei sempre desta. Anche oggi che è sonno
> universale.
>
> [*You're there, under a gravestone. Awakening you is no good /
> because you're always awake. Even today, a day of universal / sleep.*]

'Nel silenzio' is by no means one of the more impressive poems in the book. It nakedly exemplifies a rhetorical structure which recurs frequently in *Satura*, a playing with *vers libre* discourse which is far removed from the austere poetry of Montale's earlier books. Perhaps the poet is carrying out his own suggestion (made in a lecture in Paris in 1952 on 'La solitudine dell'artista', now published in *Auto da fé*, Milan, 'Il Saggiatore', 1966 and 1971) that there should be a 'low' poetry for the ordinary reader alongside the 'high' poetry written for the initiate. Much of *Satura* in fact consists of neatly versified verbal rings run round Montale's most dearly hated ideological *clichés* or *bêtes noires*, mimicking Pasolini.

However, 'Nel silenzio' also lays bare structures that are basic to Montale's poetry and, in particular, its political structure. The strike is stripped of all political significance, indeed of all significance whatsoever, and trivialised by Montale's sardonic metaphysic as 'silenzio totale' and 'sonno/universale', to be contrasted with the dead woman as a blank negative to an existential positive.

Montale's poetry had always rested on the unreality of the 'real' world and the obscurity of the self contrasted with a tormentingly elusive 'other', which could be glimpsed, in rare and privileged moments, only in its absence or unattainability, as an undecipherable and fleeting 'barlume' in things. In the existential landscape of parched or storm-battered cliffs of Montale's first book of poems, *Ossi di seppia* (1925), the sea was the bearer of this mysterious message (signally in the 'Mediterraneo' sequence), though the same Orphic suggestions glowed in the lemons and sunflowers of other poems. In *Le Occasioni* (1939), it is the absent woman, Clizia, named after the sunflower, who bears the mysterious sign of truth and salvation to the poet. She is joined in *La Bufera, e altro* (1956, with a slightly revised second edition in 1961) by Iride and Volpe. Clizia is an angel-woman, as in the medieval poetry of the *dolce stil novo*, Iride an emanation of Christ himself.

These, then, and hardly any others, are the few shadowy human figures in Montale's poetry credited with any real existence. The rest of humanity is mentioned pityingly, if at all, as 'questa ghiacciata moltitudine di morti' ['this frozen multitude of corpses'] (*Ossi* – 'Arsenio'), though the poet frequently longs to sacrifice himself for the joy of a vague 'voi'. In the Fascist Italy of the years when Montale wrote the poems of *Ossi* and *Le Occasioni* – though his negative metaphysic is born fully-fledged in his first poem, 'Meriggiare pallido e assorto', written in 1916 – this dismissal of all but a few chosen individuals amounted to political opposition through poetry. So indeed it was taken by a whole generation of readers and writers. Montale made no secret of his contempt for Fascism and because of it lost his librarian's post and endured a precarious livelihood for years. The poems of *La Bufera* are full of allusions – mostly through the storm imagery of the title – to the nightmare of Fascism and war, and indeed the 'Finisterre' section, with its epigraph from D'Aubigné against tyranny, had to be smuggled into Switzerland for publication in 1943. Yet, until the last section of *La Bufera*, 'Conclusioni provvisorie', politics provides the explicit content for hardly any poems. The poet's revulsion against mass religious fervour largely inspires 'Elegia di Pico Farnese' in *Le Occasioni* and 'Le processioni del 1949' in *La Bufera*, while 'La primavera hitleriana', written after the war, recalls in the present tense Hitler's pre-war meeting with Mussolini in Florence.

In each poem, as in 'Nel silenzio', the saving reality of the chosen woman is invoked to cancel the squalor of the public spectacle. So in 'Le processioni del '49', the Marian devotees' 'tanfo acre che infetta / le zolle a noi devote' ['sour reek polluting/our consecrated turf'] is abolished by a ' . . . se non fosse' which leads to the triumphant affirmative:

> La tua virtù furiosamente angelica
> ha scacciato col guanto i madonnari
> pellegrini, Cibele e i Coribanti.

> [*The angel fury of your virtue / with the wave of a glove has dispelled the Madonna worshippers / on pilgrimage, Cybele and the Corybantes.*]

The oracular force of all Montale's poetry in fact depends on a metaphysical affirmative. In his 'Lettera da Albenga' of 1963 (now in *Auto da fé*, pp. 349-50), Montale claims for poetry the unique religious function of recognising the deities who walk incognito in our midst. So his poetry distinguishes the divine from the irredeemably mundane. The hostile reality is not rationally examined in moral, social or political terms. It is presented as a *physical* presence, hard to the senses, even phonetically, especially in *Ossi*, with a pervasive sense of the alienness of the sensory world. Montale's poetic method (at least until *Satura*) is animistic, attributing metaphysical qualities to physical objects, as in tribal religion. In his collection of autobiographical essays, *Farfalla di Dinard* (1966), he asserts: 'L'animismo è la posizione spirituale più degna dell'uomo e anche la più logica' ['Animism is the spiritual standpoint most worthy of man and also the most logical'], (p. 184). Thus when Montale descends into the arena of ideological discourse, in *Satura*, the fragility and arbitrariness of his attitudes become plain. His ideological poems are nearly always close to parody or derisive verbal antics, and his purpose can only be to devalue any attempt at rational discourse and to keep poetry safe for metaphysics and the tyranny of metaphor.

Umberto Carpi has carefully studied Montale's political ideology, matching the poems to the poet's essays and articles. Montale seems to have yearned for a return to a perhaps mythical *Ottocento*, a pre-industrial society of gentlefolk dedicated to culture, and to have hoped to find just this after the downfall of Fascism. This would give a political basis to Montale's metaphysic, which sees Time and the material world as the 'wrong' Time and the 'wrong' world, but the only ones we've got.

Thus the only 'real' people that inhabit Montale's world are a few individuals intimately known and loved, who, like the poet himself, are lost, fugitive, absent or dead, yet 'saved' perhaps, without even knowing it, against the existential void of the unholy world. Society, even 'high' society, exists in Montale's poetry only as horde or ant-hill. Once individuals form part of a social group other than that of the manorial or patrician household ('i miei morti, / i miei cani fidati, le mie vecchie / serve' ['my dead, / my trusty dogs, my old / serving-women'], in 'L'arca' from *La Bufera*) they are beyond Montale's will to understand. Not that Montale would disagree with Fortini's realisation that 'La salvezza individuale è il piú abbietto dei privilegi', ['Individual salvation is the most abject of privileges']. On the contrary, 'per tutti' is a phrase frequently applied to the mystical self-sacrifice of the poet or of Clizia. If, with the Volpe poems of sections IV and VI of *La Bufera*, and subsequently, Montale discovers that 'il dono che sognavo / non per me ma per tutti / appartiene a me solo' ['the gift I dreamt of / not for me but for everyone / belongs to me alone'] ('Anniversario', *La Bufera*), he implies that this is because 'history', the mass of mankind, has gone another way, and he bears witness to his own steadfastness, rejecting the 'lume di chiesa o d'officina / che alimenti / chierico rosso, o nero', ['church-light or shop-floor light / fed / by the cleric in red, or in black'] in the sombre 'Piccolo Testamento'. Montale, in fact, could not stand being for long even in the Partito d'Azione. He managed to avoid military service in 1940 but was not active in the Resistance. Nominated senator in 1967, he declared himself outside all parties but has since supported the

Liberals, the anti-clerical and anti-Marxist party of high finance and big business. In 'Il sogno del prigioniero' (also in *La Bufera*), he sees little to choose between Fascism and its successor regime: 'Albe e notti qui variano per pochi segni', ['Dawns and nights differ here by few signs']. Power is unchanging and irrational: 'La purga dura da sempre, senza un perché', ['The purge has always gone on, without reason']. There are clear allusions to Hitler and Stalin ('questo sterminio d'oche'), ['this slaughter of geese'] and those who wield power are characterised metaphysically, but with hackneyed rhetoric, as 'Iddii pestilenziali' ['pestilential Gods'].

If Montale's poetry is irrational, devoid of any insight into social or political processes, perhaps that is because of the fact that he faces two irreducible political realities in society: the irrational endurance of Power (translated, in everyday life, into 'economic determinism') and the unrationalisable endurance of the suffering, alienated self. Had Montale been able to resolve his metaphysical dichotomy of the impossible into the epic poetry of the possible, then he would be the great poet of our age. But this is an idle might-have-been. The literary tradition to which (as Carpi has shown) he always kept allegiance could not accommodate such a vast modern vision. He remains one of the noblest poets of that tradition.

## Giuseppe Tomasi di Lampedusa's *Il Gattopardo:* the owl of Minerva

> When philosophy paints its gloomy picture a form of life has grown old. It cannot be rejuvenated by the gloomy picture, but only understood. Only when dusk starts to fall does the owl of Minerva spread its wings and fly.

Hegel's words could have been written of *Il gattopardo*. There can hardly be a literary work, even a historical novel, so steeped in historicism or a novelist, since Scott, with such 'insopprimibili tendenze storiografiche', in the deepest and broadest sense, as Lampedusa. No novelist has shown with such sophisticated awareness and precision, and with such a tragic sense of human betrayal and self-betrayal, the shifts of class supremacy and the changing forms and methods of economic, political and social control. A Hegelian 'Cunning of Reason' (or a Marxian 'development in the relations of production and exchange') uses people to make history, but not as they would

25

like to make it. History itself, not the Zeus-like Prince Fabrizio Salina, is the protagonist of *Il gattopardo*, as it is in any true historical novel. The book's chapter-titles are dates.

It may indeed appear that history provides the background rather than the foreground of the novel, even though the events themselves – the passing of the Bourbon Kingdom of the Two Sicilies – seal the tomb of eight hundred years of feudalism. True, we witness no battles. We do not meet Garibaldi. The 'action' of the school history-books is merely reported as hearsay. Fabrizio keeps out of it. But he cannot keep out of history. He in fact makes the historic decisions, even when he thinks he is abstaining from history. He advises the people of Donnafugata to vote for Unification; he arranges for Tancredi to marry the wealthy, beautiful but plebeian Angelica rather than his daughter Concetta, who is as fond of Tancredi as he is of her, and thus gives away what is left of his family's future; in the famous meeting with Chevalley, he turns down the offer of a seat on the new Senate and recommends Angelica's father, Sedàra, instead. He has power, which he abdicates. Fabrizio, described as the most intelligent member of his class, 'stava a contemplare la rovina del proprio ceto e del proprio patrimonio senza avere nessuna attività ed ancora minor voglia di porvi riparo' (p.21) ['looked on at the ruin of his own class and his own birthright without doing anything and with even less inclination to stem the tide'].

In an essay on the links between literature and politics in Italy today, one cannot avoid mention of the politico-literary hullabaloo that accompanied the novel's unique sales success. Left-wing critics rushed to attack it as a nostalgic apology for aristocracy and a denial of history, of the possibility of real change or progress, in Sicily or anywhere else. Those who defended the novel were usually equally. misled and disingenuously partisan. Anglophone critics, too, have generally preferred to disguise their conscious or unconscious political instincts in the spotless robe of 'pure' aesthetic analysis or of existential individualism – and this despite Lampedusa's continual insistence on the social and political issues in explicit class terms.

Yet Louis Aragon has claimed that Lampedusa has followed his favourite novelist, Stendhal, in producing a left-wing critique of his own class. Most critics – *gattopardeschi* or *anti-gattopardeschi* – have rather naively lifted out Fabrizio's extemporised statement to Chevalley of his 'philosophy' of geographical and social determinism and Sicilian immobility as if it were *the* philosophy of the book, of the

author, and of history itself. Chevalley's own presence contradicts
this. So does the figure of the self-made man, Sedàra, with whom the
future lies; and Fabrizio contradicts himself, on the subject of Sicilian
inertia, by proposing Sedàra's name, rather than his own, for the
Senate. It is clear that what Fabrizio says of Sicily is only true of
himself and most of his class. It is not even true of the whole of his
class, as his nephew Tancredi proves, not to mention Fabrizio's own
son, Giovanni, who has escaped to be a coal-merchant's clerk in
London.

It is a paradox of Lampedusa's art (and not of his alone), and
perhaps its main weakness, that misinterpretation of his book should
be at one and the same time a tribute to his skill in making a living
character of Fabrizio and a token of his failure to put Fabrizio into
clear perspective. The paradox makes itself evident in the book's
unresolved technical difficulties, which arise from the problem of
reconciling the method of narrating by 'point of view' or 'interior
monologue' (Lampedusa uses this latter term himself in his *Lezioni su
Stendhal*) with that of 'omniscience' ('il metodo di far narrare la storia
da Dio' ['the method of having the story told by God'], to quote the
same source).

Fabrizio's 'point of view' does not extend over the whole novel. It is
not even absolute and continuous in those sections which it covers.
Yet such is the power of the characterisation that Fabrizio's presence
tends to fill the whole novel and overwhelm it, and his brilliance
almost conceals his incompetence.

Lampedusa attempts to keep his protagonist within bounds by the
use of an omniscience which is not that of God but that of history. He
fails largely because of the fascinating complexity of his character:
Fabrizio frequently anticipates (if only by the chance shifts of his
reflective intelligence) both the future course of history and history's
judgment of himself and his times – just as frequently as he mistakes
both; he also frequently anticipates the author's, or the reader's,
moral judgments of him. Fabrizio thus tends to disarm both history
and ethics. He can quote Baudelaire (anonymously):

> . . . donnez-moi la force et le courage
> de regarder mon coeur et mon corps sans dégoût (p. 40)

but it is always true of him that, as when he shoots a rabbit, he enjoys
'in aggiunta al piacere di uccidere, anche quello rassicurante di com-
patire' (p. 126) ['in addition to the pleasure of killing, the reassuring

pleasure of pitying as well']. So Fabrizio's uneasiness over the political turn of events leads him to discover the sham of the new 'democracy':

> . . . adesso sapeva chi era stato ucciso a Donnafugata, in cento altri luoghi, nel corso di quella nottata di vento lercio: una neonata: la buonafede. . . . (p. 137)
> [ . . . *now he knew who had been killed in Donnafugata, in a hundred other places, in the course of that night of foul wind: a new-born infant: good faith.* . . . ]

But, as always, his self-indulgent moralism enables him to conceal his own responsibility from himself, as from so many of his readers. He arranges a matrimonial alliance with the very man who has strangled the new liberties at birth and makes over his seat on the Italian Senate to the same man. It is the omniscience of Lampedusa's historical hindsight that explicitly steps in to correct the false perspective that Fabrizio is shortly to put before Chevalley:

> Don Fabrizio non poteva saperlo allora, ma una buona parte della neghittosità, dell'acquiescenza per la quale durante i decenni seguenti si doveva vituperare la gente del Mezzogiorno, ebbe la propria origine nello stupido annullamento della prima espressione di libertà che a questi si fosse mai presentata. (pp. 139-140)
> [*Don Fabrizio could not have known it at the time, but a good part of the inertia, the servility for which the people of the South were to be reviled during the ensuing decades, had its origins in the senseless annulment of the first expression of liberty which opportunity had ever allowed them.*]

This frequently clumsy intrusion of the historian upon the narrator is one of the least artistically successful of a number of devices which Lampedusa uses to establish a critical detachment of the reader from his protagonist – devices which, in Brechtian terms, might be called *Verfremdungseffekten*. Most notable of these are the chapters which revolve around other 'centres of consciousness' – Padre Pirrone's in the fifth chapter and Concetta's in the last. The extended time-span of the novel also emphasises the irony of history.

Still, these devices only emphasise what is already discernible through Fabrizio's own 'interior monologues': his bullying of his family and dependents; his weakness for Tancredi and Angelica; his neglect of his affairs; his betrayal of his family, of the values he purports to stand for, of himself, to one of the men he despises most.

The crumbling of his estate and his class– so splendidly and discreetly suggested throughout the novel by the significant interplay of concrete details– is made by him to appear to himself and the reader as the inexorable work of Time and Death, as part of the deterministic, naturalistic rise and fall of civilisations, while all along he makes or avoids decisions which, within their measure of freedom (and, for a Sicilian Prince in 1860, it is a considerable one), help to determine the specific features of a political system. He *chooses* to fulfil the economic determinism advocated by the new capitalist hegemony represented by Sedàra.

And this brings us back to the present. For many have seen the parallel between the Risorgimento, with its unfulfilled promise, and the Resistance and its equally disappointing fruits. Numerous allusions suggest such a parallelism in the novel, and the emphasis on clerical influence in the final chapter is only too pointed.

'Se vogliamo che tutto rimanga come è, bisogna che tutto cambi.' ['If we want everything to stay as it is, everything has to change.'] Tancredi's paradox, which subtends the whole novel and could well be the historical judgment of the novel, beyond the intentions of its protagonists, cuts with both edges. Like Pareto's and Mosca's analyses of ruling groups, which the whole novel so closely echoes, it demystifies the historical transmission of power.

## Ignazio Silone: the adventure of a poor socialist

Alone among Italian writers of this century, Silone was active in the front line of politics before he came to literature. Caught between the traps of the reformist Socialism of the Second International and the Leninism of the Third International, Silone found himself on the far left, opposed in varying degrees to Fascists, clericals, capitalists, liberals, reformists and Communists– in short, to all 'systems'. In our contemporary politics, this stance means impotence, and writing is Silone's way out of that impotence– a direct address to the people. His 'reading-public' (as Luce D'Eramo tells us) includes peasants engaged in political struggle in many parts of the world, as well as people in Italy's country towns who are normally quite unconcerned by merely literary events.

Silone was a revolutionary from his 'teens and, at the age of twenty-one, as leader of the Socialist youth movement, helped to found the Italian Communist Party. He continued in the Italian

29

Communist leadership after all opposition to Fascism had been driven underground in 1925 and was present at the meeting of the Comintern in Moscow in 1927 when Stalin ousted Zinoviev and Trotsky. This experience Silone describes in *Uscita di sicurezza* (1949, but republished in 1965 in the volume entitled after it). It was the experience that led to Silone's disaffection towards Communism, which he had embraced as the only effective form of struggle against oppression but which he now increasingly saw as a new mode of oppression.

*Uscita di sicurezza*, together with the other memoirs and essays in the volume, is one of the most moving and serious political autobiographies of our age. Many things in it are memorable: all centre on the spectacle of a whole person, Secondo Tranquilli (as Silone was called before Fascist persecution made him take an alias), bravely trying to face the moral – that is, the political – problems of his society with a steadfastness summed up in his daily prayer as a pupil in a religious school: 'Mio Dio, aiutami a vivere senza tradire' ['My God, help me to live without betraying'] (p. 80). This determination not to betray led Silone to identify with the down-trodden peasantry of his native Marsica, a mountainous district in the Abruzzi, and to place his peasantry at the heart of all his imaginative writing. All his writing shows that the age-old oppression of the peasantry existed long before Fascism and that Fascism was already implicit in Italy's ruling classes, becoming explicit as a reaction to the political organisation of peasants and workers. The sardonic dialogues of *La scuola dei dittatori*, which appeared in 1938 and was republished in a revised form in 1962, illustrate from history the ease with which Fascism can arise in any modern society.

*Uscita* also explains, if explanation were needed, the Christian element in Silone's work. Christianity was part of the life of the Italian peasantry. The peasants necessarily expressed their Christianity in revolutionary terms and their revolution in Christian terms. This is most vividly imaged in the peasant Lazzaro's picture of the Red Christ (*Uscita di sicurezza*, p. 147). Silone spells out his views in the introductory essays to *L'avventura d'un povero cristiano* (1968): his is a Christianity 'ridotto alla sua sostanza morale' (p. 41) ['reduced to its moral substance'].

In Italy, the peasantry has shrunk to a minority, almost a marginal section of the population – though it seems likely that there will long remain a down-trodden rural labour force. In many parts of the world, the peasantry can still expect a long and probably hard future as the majority of the population. Silone, in his preface to *Fontamara* (1933, with a revised edition in 1949), expressly declares that he writes for all the world's peasantry. It is a great disservice to reduce him (or Vittorini, or Pavese), as Jürgen Rühle does in 'Italy between Black and Red', in his book *Literature and Revolution* (pp. 365-85), to a local patriot preaching 'small kindnesses' (see pp. 371-2). Silone expressly rejects provincialism (in *L'avventura*, see pp. 33-4) and is nowhere guilty of fatuous local chauvinism. He is unequivocally an international revolutionary baffled by the power of the modern bureaucratic state – whether parliamentary reformist or Soviet or otherwise nakedly authoritarian in its class supremacy– to drug people into inert dependence and the most inane form of individualism (which, of course, amounts to conformism). This is the theme of 'Ripensare il progresso', the long last essay in *Uscita di sicurezza*. It is also the main theme of his Brechtian stage-parable, *L'avventura d'un povero cristiano*: the monk who thinks he can change the Church by becoming head of its bureaucracy as Pope Celestine V admits total failure. Much of the play consists of dark comic satire of the straw men who embody the system: the village priest, the gendarme, the local magistrate in the country scenes; and, at the Papal court, the Pope's secretary and the prelates. The only fully human beings are the small band of persecuted dissenters and their peasant friends.

*L'avventura* is set nearly seven centuries before the welfare society of 'Ripensare il progresso' and differs from the latter in a crucial respect: in the play, the presence of the people thirsting for truth and justice is always felt, particularly in Part IV, where all the country folk affect to have lost their voices rather than act as town-criers to announce that there is a price on the head of the fugitive ex-Pope – while the knave and buffoon, Cerbicca, turns the job into a mockery of the authorities. The people, ordinary folk, it can be argued, are the real, if inconspicuous, heroes and subjects of the play, and Pier Celestino, the 'povero cristiano', is their voice, politically inaudible even when installed at the centre of power.

The peasantry is quite plainly the collective hero of *Fontamara*, as Jean Whyte has well observed. They are insultingly called *cafoni*, but Silone's introduction makes the word a symbol of slighted human dignity. (*Il segreto di Luca* centres on the discovery that a *cafone* is capable of the noblest love.) *Fontamara* is a hybrid: it makes up for being a novel by being also a folk-epic. It is a collective characterisation of the peasantry by themselves. Individuals, whether from the

31

peasantry or from their oppressors, are seen as the several, distinct faces of a social class. The peasants are shown in all their brutalised ignorance and mean egoisms – ignorance and egoisms which are nothing to the barbarity and rapacity of the educated gentry and civilised townsfolk who appropriate the peasants' water-supply, terrorise them, carry out a group rape, and, when the villagers at last begin to organise resistance, wipe out the village. It is a pattern familiar to peasants round the world. So is the petty everyday oppression, such as when Don Abbacchio raises his fees for administering the sacraments or Donna Clorinda checks the size of the eggs which the peasant women bring her as gifts.

The larger-than-life humour and despair of the peasants' outlook are what establish their humanity in spite of all their faults. This epic breadth of outlook derives naturally from each individual's sense of belonging to the peasant community as a whole – in fact, from his class solidarity. (Berardo Viola's discovery of *l'amicizia* in the novel is the explicit articulation of this.) The peasant philosophy is expressed in a whole range of drily preposterous fables about God and the saints and their dealings with the peasants. The devil, too, is made to play his part and is held to blame for the unaccountable burning of the landowners' hay-ricks and fences. Thus, their religious superstition can work for the *cafoni*, as during the first Fascist raid, when the blackshirts are put to flight by the appearance of the Madonna in the belfry (actually Elvira).

There is much more in this unique book than we have space to indicate. It is, continuously, both preposterously funny and harrowing. Its power cannot be explained in the usual aesthetic terms, but by the unnerving, literal gravity of what it says – that is, by an aesthetic quality of a different order. In contrast, *Il segreto di Luca* (1956) and particularly *La volpe e le camelie* (1960), which most obviously display conventional narrative skills, are undoubtedly Silone's weakest novels.

*Fontamara* showed both the peasants' total lack of political consciousness and the tragic cost of revolt under Fascism. Silone's successive novels strive to overcome this double problem. It is the central problem of revolutionary politics, and therefore the revolutionary activist from now on becomes the immediate focus of attention. This makes the later books less like epic and more like novels, and they have won more favour among critics. The protagonist's reflective individual conscience encourages identification by the educated reader, and, indeed, the interest of these books, though different from that of *Fontamara*, is neither superficial nor accidental. The revolutionary Pietro Spina's disguise as a priest in *Vino e pane* (1955, but first published as *Pane e vino* in 1936) and his secret barn-commune of animal and human oddities in *Il seme sotto la neve* (1941 and 1961) are both extraordinarily imaginative ways of revealing the difficulties of setting up a free and just community among a Godforsaken peasantry under a vicious political regime. For swiftness and liveliness of penetration – social, political and moral – of rural and provincial life these books surpass all the laborious and prosy endeavours of *neorealismo*.

*Una manciata di more* (1952) is set after the downfall of Fascism, when at least formal political freedoms have been restored and the peasants form their own Soviet so as to reclaim their lands from the gentry: the main threat now comes from the Party (Communist), which seeks to capture the peasant movement. Rocco, like Silone and Pietro Spina, leaves the Party and joins the peasants. The novel thus reflects the political turmoil and intrigue of the agrarian agitation following the Liberation. But it does not, any more than Silone's other works, solve the problem which Silone saw as the overriding one of our age and of every age: the problem of realising utopia (*L'avventura*, p. 30), a genuinely human community, especially in the face of the ever-increasing encroachments of bureaucratic power. The more or less invisible community of companions which exists in all Silone's works never amounts to more than a tiny dissenting minority, too ascetic and informal to break down the massive structures of our profane society. For a utopian Christian, Silone is not enough of a visionary, but he has broken through the usual bounds of 'literature' to speak seriously to people to whom 'literature' usually has nothing to say.


## Guareschi's microcosm: politics as play

Giovanni Guareschi's immensely popular 'Mondo Piccolo' books daringly transform the struggle between the Catholic Church and Communism in rural Italy. In these books, Italy's political battles are fought out in miniature, and with enormous gusto, by Don Camillo, the parish priest of a small Po-side town, and Peppone, the Communist mayor. It is Guareschi's brilliant invention to make Peppone *almost* Camillo's equal in strength, courage and guile and, to all intents and purposes, his brother. They are sworn political enemies, but each of them has a heart of gold. Not only do they covertly help each other out, but Peppone and his fellow 'Reds', for all their denunciations of religion, war, capitalism, marriage, patriotism, turn out in a series of highly comic narrative episodes to have been war-heroes or secretly married to their brazen 'kept' women; to be commercially minded; to want their children baptised; to light votive candles to the madonna; to defend their statues of angels, saints and the madonna with fierce jealousy; and to be stubbornly loyal to their parish priest. Political conflict is thus ritualised into a game in which the comedy – and often the pathos – depends on the two supposed antagonists turning out to be on the same side.

Both the figures and the landscape of this miniature rustic battle-field become larger than life in Guareschi's narration, which draws largely on the folk imagination. The heroic stature of Camillo and Peppone and the rest is matched and enhanced by the dominating presence of the mighty river Po, the deity which presides over this folk-world, giving the land its abundant fertility but also threatening terror and destruction with its periodic floods.

As in folk-literature, everything is externalised, translated with remarkable economy into swift action or into the equally dynamic cut-and-thrust of dialogue. This leads Guareschi to another bold stroke. He presents Camillo as conversing with the crucified Christ on the altar. Thus Camillo acquires a degree of inwardness which cannot fully emerge in his role-playing with Peppone. It is also another device (offering more comic opportunities) by which Guareschi partly transcends political partisanship, for Christ's voice is that of Camillo's conscience and of universal love.

The device of the talking Christ also fits in with the folk religion of the 'Mondo Piccolo' books, which concretises the sacramental into objects (statues of saints, angels, the madonna, and, to some extent, the crucifix itself), rituals (the Mass, christenings, weddings and other sacraments, processions and blessings of the river-waters or the fields), persons (the priest Don Camillo and his aged and indomitable bishop), and buildings (the parish church). All these are regarded fetishistically as *property* – common property, to be fiercely defended. Christ's voice may tell Camillo that statues, even the crucifix, are meaningless objects in themselves, but, as Camillo replies on one occasion (in the first 'Mondo Piccolo' collection, called simply *Don*

*Camillo*, 1948), 'Voi conoscete l'umanità, ma io conosco gli italiani', ['You know mankind, but I know the Italians']. In any case, Guareschi does not show us the sacramental illuminating the people's lives from within, and the priest retains his traditional unique authority as minister of the sacramental, mediating between God and man. Only Don Camillo hears Christ's voice.

Guareschi has thus used the devices of popular literature to convey a clear political message of fraternal acceptance of the Communists in so far as they in their turn accept traditional Church authority and renounce revolution (in fact, if not in theory). This may seem surprising, as Guareschi was outspokenly anti-Communist. Indeed, he claimed, in his preface to *Il compagno Don Camillo* (1963), that his humorous and satirical political weekly, *Candido* (where the 'Mondo Piccolo' series had started life as a regular column), had helped to keep the Communists out of power in the 1948 Italian election.

The 'Mondo Piccolo' stories do sometimes present a shadowy sort of Communist quite different from Peppone and his comrades: the sinister grey eminences of the Party – thugs, fanatics and hard-line Stalinists. Christ's voice is silent about their sort. They are the personification of evil: alien, incomprehensible, unredeemable. Their murderous schemes are always forestalled by Peppone or Don Camillo, in stories which Guareschi bases on the rumours which were circulating in Italy between the period of the Resistance and the 1948 elections, about secret hoards of Communist arms and an imminent uprising.

So far Guareschi seems clear: Communism with the Church and without revolution – yes; otherwise – no. He supports this perspective, however, by avoiding most of Italy's real historic problems. The crimes committed by Fascism with the connivance of the Church are never mentioned, nor is the bloody civil war in Mussolini's German-protected North Italian 'Social Republic'. Nor is the depopulation and neglect of much of the countryside. The facts of Emilian life and of Guareschi's own life contradict the perspective he offers. The Emilia of Don Camillo and Guareschi is a traditional Red stronghold, and, ironically, the main reason why it still lends itself to idyllic treatment as a 'Mondo Piccolo', a viable peasant community, is its co-operative social infrastructure; while, for his part, Guareschi makes no mention of religion in his autobiographical works – and he became a city-dweller. Thus, political geography and history, and Guareschi's own life and literary output as a whole, show up the

35

'Mondo Piccolo's' surface message of rural Catholic populism as being not a social and ethical reality but folk memory or myth, as the very designation 'Mondo Piccolo' implies.

But the 'Mondo Piccolo' is not insulated from the historical movement of the modern world and contains its own self-transforming inner dialectic, as involuntary on Guareschi's part as the outer dialectic we have just remarked upon. Peppone's Communist ideology appears in a comic or ironic light, as the garb of an illusory persona which can never conceal Peppone's 'real' nature as an Italian Catholic. Yet Guareschi states that ideology with an eloquent rationality which outlasts its own comic or ironic unfulfilment. Indeed, in *Il compagno Don Camillo*, it is Don Camillo who sarcastically delivers a Marxist critique of Peppone's bourgeois weakness in succumbing to the capitalist lure of gambling on the football pools and wanting to turn the prize-money into a lucrative investment. The ideological point is crystallised in an intense narrative image: Peppone and his wife creep into Don Camillo's presbytery (where he is keeping the money for them) at dead of night, bursting to see what such a huge sum of money looks like.

Don Camillo uses the secret of Peppone's pools win to blackmail him into including Camillo in a party of Italian comrades visiting the Soviet Union. Not only does the priest become 'compagno' Camillo Tarocci, with a collapsible crucifix disguised as a fountain-pen and his breviary bound in red and renamed *Maxims of Lenin*; he is ideologically disguised also, showing a complete command of Party doctrine, which he uses devastatingly to cause disarray in the ranks of the Italian comrades. The dialectic is the same as before: most of the professed comrades turn out to be happily unregenerate Italians after all. Soviet reality, on the other hand, is shown to be dismally inferior to its own aspirations. It represents the contradiction and the real absence of its own ideology at the same time as it represents, to Guareschi, the absence of God. But again, the ideology eloquently stated by 'comrade' Camillo, with ironic intent, survives its own non-realisation by the very State which professes that same ideology. In fact, Guareschi treats Soviet life with journalistic superficiality. He economically type-characterises comrade Oregov as the personification of the system, a man out of Christ's reach, who finally, while everyone else is kneeling before Don Camillo's crucifix during a storm at sea, falls overboard and drowns. Rarely is Guareschi's God so obviously *ex machina*.

36

In *Don Camillo e i giovani d'oggi* (1969), the dialectical role of ideology is even more potently taken up by the younger generation, Camillo and Peppone remaining more in the background. Peppone's long-haired son, Michele, who leads the local motor-bike gang, and Camillo's niece, Flora, who rides with the motor-bike gang from the nearest town, are made of the same epic stuff as their elders and accomplish equally hair-raising and comic exploits, as they roar out the infectious rhetoric of the Youth International against the rotten, hypocritical, inhuman world of their elders. But of course they have hearts of gold, too, and eventually make their peace with that world in a handsome church wedding. And, as before, the resonance of their moral fervour outlasts the ironic reversals to which the fervour is subjected. The profoundest comedy in the book comes when Flora pretends to be pregnant by Peppone's son and extracts large sums of money from both Don Camillo and Peppone by threatening a scandal. Their moral misery is that of their society, and the comedy lies in Flora's playing on the 'rules' of her elders' sham morality.

But this time Guareschi's unintentional dialectic is even more out of control, just as he has become more than ever a perceptive chronicler of our times. There is an infectious cynicism in Flora's deal with Peppone, a reflection in miniature of modern marketing operations: she sells refrigerators in secret partnership with Peppone, while pretending to be a cut-throat competitor. Her brazenly feminine sales technique compels an ambiguous delight, and Christ's voice, forcibly pressed into the narrative to deliver a long moral sermon against 'modern materialism' which threatens to engulf Faith, cannot carry much conviction. Guareschi's traditional Catholicism lacks notions adequate for a counter-rationale to the workings of the consumer society and remains caught between cynical acceptance in fact and total rejection in theory. It clings to semblances, in terror of the authentic. Guareschi's contradictory populism is impotent at the level of ideas; at the level of art, it does not lack imaginative and comic vigour and often transcends its own surface intentions.

## Cesare Pavese: from literature to suicide

Literature and suicide were Pavese's twin vocations from youth. His diary, *Il mestiere di vivere* (1952), documents their progress and diagnoses the ambiguous role of literature as virus ['il voluttuoso'] and

37

possible cure (see the entry for 20 April 1936, p. 43). Pavese appends two essays to the poems of *Lavorare stanca* (originally published in 1936) showing that his rejection of 'il voluttuoso' – the autobiographical exclusiveness and pointless virtuosity then prevailing in Italian poetry – had been illusory and had led him into a new 'voluttuoso'. This literary struggle with himself ended only with his suicide.

If politics are our relationships with one another, their supreme aim, therefore, being to serve all individuals not as abstract and separate entities but in their mutual relations, the incommunicable individual that Pavese presents is both politically incapable and one of the most intractable of political problems. Modern literature is full of intellectuals anguished at losing their social roots and their grip on reality. What saves Pavese's narrative works from banality is the awful unemphaticness with which he takes his ideological alternatives – morality, myth and destiny, politics and history – to their deadly conclusions.

His hopeless protagonists, then, appear almost in a social vacuum, their origins often having a validity more symbolic than naturalistic, as in the case of the foundling Anguilla in *La luna e i falò* (1950). Pavese omits the social and political dimension of loneliness. The sexual, psychological and existential dimensions generally prevail. Although Pavese sees adult experience as essentially a *reliving* of key moments of one's infancy, he avoids exploring infancy and the pressures upon it of that powerful societal microcosm – the family.

Pavese's notions of politics and society were, in fact, scanty. He spent his youth in Turin as an inactive anti-Fascist and a friend of active anti-Fascists. This latter association brought him a year's exile, in 1935-6, to Brancaleone, on the Ionian Sea. His diary, begun there, makes no mention of politics during his exile. After his return to Turin, his diary pays more attention to politics, but mainly to confess his own political nihilism, which passes for liberalism (p. 178, entry for 8 or 9 January 1940; see also the entries for June and July 1940, especially p. 199). The crucial year 1944 saw him taking refuge from the civil war in the Piedmontese hills at Serralunga di Crea: his diary over this period is concerned exclusively with God, myth and past literature.

In 1945, Pavese emerged from his seclusion into the heady air of the Liberation and belatedly joined the Communist Party, of which he remained a member until his death, though his Party activity, diligent for a few years, had dwindled to nothing by 1950. Having tried God without lasting results, he was to have the same experience with Communism, adding to his burden of confusion and guilt a 'responsabilità politica, che mi schiaccia' ['political responsibility which crushes me'] (*Il mestiere di vivere*, p. 402, entry for 27 May 1950).

In Pavese's fiction, too, politics gradually build up into a major tension in the individual's predicament. (We need not labour here the sympathy with which Pavese treats the working world as opposed to the corrupt and idle rich – a mark of his *comunismo del cuore*.) His most 'committed' novel, pointedly entitled *Il compagno* (1947), is generally reckoned to be his weakest. The first half is typically Pavesian. The feckless Pablo is contrasted with his friend Amelio who (like Nuto in *La luna e i falò* and the anti-Fascist workers in *La casa in collina*) has a quiet sense of his own and other people's dignity and who is light-hearted and steadfast. Pablo's admiration for Amelio turns into a miserable sense of guilt and inferiority as he first takes Linda from his friend, now disabled, and then fails to win her.

This reflects Pavese's oft-reiterated belief in the fixity of character, in the impossibility of changing oneself; the belief that we are adults from birth, or else life-long adolescents. There is a political contrast between the smart and desirable but fickle and faithless woman and the loyal, available, but uninteresting one: the former, the ambitious Linda, gravitates towards the tycoon, Lubrani, and the Fascist establishment; the latter, Gina, is, in this book, accepted by Pablo, and, with her, the working-class ethic of the Communist *compagno*. In every other novel, Pavese's theme is the inability of his autobiographical protagonist to commit himself to the people and to the cause which he knows to be the better one. This is what explains Corrado's respect for the Fascist dead in the celebrated ending of *La casa in collina* (1949). They at least *have* committed themselves.

Many criticisms have been made of the second half of *Il compagno*: Pablo's adherence to the anti-Fascist cause seems to take place almost casually, by a mere change of place from Turin to Rome; his motives – the desire to emulate Amelio and to be revenged on Linda – are not apparently political; the Roman section is more of an adventure than a political experience; the problem of maturing has been dismissed rather than solved. Some of these criticisms are certainly more valid than others, but the theme of true 'comradeship' as a paradise where the simply human and the political meet is implied though not depicted in much of Pavese's writing: the possibility of gaining this paradise within oneself needed to be outlined, but in *Il compagno*

Pavese impoverished the theme with too much incompetent detail. Certainly, class struggle seems almost the last of Pavese's concerns, and he throws little light upon it.

It is significant that *Il compagno* is the only one of Pavese's explicitly political novels which markedly contradicts his own experience: it comes dangerously close to a false epic heroism by projecting the author's political commitment, which came only after the downfall of Fascism, back to the days of the underground struggle. A post-war version of *Il compagno* would indeed be interesting.

In other novels, fiction is substantially faithful to autobiography. *Il carcere* sees the protagonist indifferent to his fellow-exile and local dissidents and immured instead in his 'prison' of desire for the forbidden female and impatience towards the clinging female. In *La casa in collina*, Corrado's hilltop lodgings symbolise his 'illusion' of detachment from politics: though he is safe while the air-raids ravage Turin, he finds that the civil war follows him up to his hilltop. The family with whom he lodges are Fascist supporters, while the workers who come to escape the air-raids are anti-Fascists preparing for insurrection; among them is Cate, an abandoned lover of Corrado's. She acquired her political principles from him and now has a young son who may be his. Cate will die, at the hands of the Nazis and Fascists, without confirming Corrado's paternity, while all Corrado can do, like Pavese himself, is to take refuge in a religious institution. Even then, the boy Dino will run away to join the partisans, while Corrado heads for a safer place.

Throughout, Pavese chastises himself mercilessly in Corrado, showing up his inadequacies, his pusillanimity, in politics as in love. The end of chapter ten marks his realisation that ' . . . con ciascuno dicevo cose opposte, cercavo sempre di sembrare un altro' [' . . . I said different things to each person, I kept trying to seem a different person'] and that what for others is a matter of life and death, he, a comfortable if lonely school-teacher, can only play at. Absolving himself repeatedly of the responsibility to act, to choose, he finally comes face to face with the Fascist militiamen killed in an ambush.

*La luna e i falò*, Pavese's last work, also ends with a killing, a killing this time much nearer to the soul's quick of the protagonist, Anguilla: it is the almost ceremonial killing by the partisans of a girl who had betrayed them to the other side, and the girl is the dazzling, disdainful Santa, a prized memory of Anguilla's boyhood. Political non-participation is rendered this time in general terms: Anguilla, of unknown parentage, has missed the civil war in northern Italy through having emigrated to the United States. That is, his non-participation has been total and, as he discovers on his return, irremediable; he has lost his past. Nuto is the man he should have become; Cinto, the boy who might become either Nuto or Anguilla.

Much in these novels consists of Pavese's confession of betrayal and self-betrayal, indicated in the joint title *Prima che il gallo canti* which he gave to *Il carcere* and *La casa in collina*. But the process that comprehends all his works is not so much confession as self-recognition, with all that the word implies about an unchangeable self and character as destiny. This is conveyed not only by the events of the narrative but by its slightly mannered and obsessive symbolic images and patterning.

In the novels, all this is set against a specific situation in place and time, in history, and the individual destined to life-long adolescence is set against other individuals otherwise 'destined'. The adolescent's destiny is quite differently, and self-pityingly, mythologised and generalised in the *Dialoghi con Leucò* (1947), the most direct fruit of Pavese's long interest in primitive religion and myth. *Dialoghi* was written at the same time as *Il compagno* and was Pavese's favourite book. It was beside him when he died.

He had failed to find, or to invent, the politics which would overcome the 'predestined' self-isolation which literature could only confirm.

## Pier Paolo Pasolini: after Eros

In the essays he collected in *Passione e ideologia* (1960) and *Empirismo eretico* (1972), Pasolini showed himself to be militantly aware of style as the very essence of political commitment in literature; of the implications of using dialect or standard Italian, of *monolinguismo* and *plurilinguismo*; of technology as the possible basis for the emergence, at last, of a truly national language in Italy (as opposed to the literary language which few Italians have ever spoken). His criteria for a popular *literary* style – as stated in his 1957 essay 'La confusione degli stili' – exactly fit Guareschi, and this highlights the simplistic way in which Pasolini used his Gramscian premise of a truly popular national literature (as well as confirming that Guareschi was closer to the literary policy of the Communist Party than were most Marxist

41

writers). Guareschi's case also illustrates the fact that writing *follows* rather than brings about changes in society – particularly changes in levels of literacy and in the literary class itself and in the technology of communication and entertainment. Pasolini's own creative writing could not be more unlike Guareschi's.

Pasolini spent much of his early life, including the historic years 1943 to 1949, in the countryside of the Friulan plain. The Friuli meant, to Pasolini, the innocence of childhood sexuality and folk religion but also an awakening to history and its conflicts through the death of his brother in the Resistance and also through the peasant agitation which drew Pasolini into the Communist Party for the year 1947-8. Sweet, sinful innocence is the burden of the intense Provençal lyricism of his exquisite poems in Friulan, collected in *La meglio gioventù* (Sansoni, 1954). The awakening to history is rendered, subjectively, in the Italian poems of *L'usignolo della Chiesa cattolica*, also written between 1943 and 1949 but not published until 1958; and, more objectively, in the novel of the peasant movement, *Il sogno di una cosa* (published in 1962, but written ten years earlier). Both these contain in germ the conflict which Pasolini was never to transcend, though he did transform its terms: on the one hand, the instinctual, the carnal, the exquisite, the private or all these together projected into an almost mystically loved archaic peasantry, Friulan, Calabrian, African or Asian or the Roman riff-raff; and, on the other hand, the rational, the civic, Marx and Gramsci and the promise of a new world – the conflict between *passione* and *ideologia*.

Love-hate is therefore Pasolini's attitude to both bourgeoisie *and* historic working class, Catholicism *and* Communism. In the celebrated long poem *Le ceneri di Gramsci*, published in the book of the same name in 1954, Pasolini directly expresses with greatest clarity and force (addressing the dead Gramsci):

> Lo scandalo del contraddirmi, dell'essere
> con te e contro te; con te nel cuore,
> in luce, contro te nelle buie viscere;
> del mio paterno stato traditore
> – nel pensiero, in un'ombra d'azione –
> mi so ad esso attaccato nel calore
> degli istinti, dell'estetica passione;
> attratto da una vita proletaria
> a te anteriore, è per me religione
> la sua allegria, non la millenaria

sua lotta: la sua natura, non la sua
coscienza . . .
. . . Ma come io possiedo la storia,
essa mi possiede; ne sono illuminato:
ma a che serve la luce?

[*The scandal of contradicting myself, of being / with you and against
you; with you in my heart, / in the light, against you in the darkness of
my guts; / traitor to my paternal state / – in thought, in a shadow of
action – / I know I cling to it in the heat / of the instincts, of my
aesthetic passions; / drawn to a proletarian life / from before your time,
my religion / is its gaiety, not its age-old / struggle: / its nature not its
consciousness . . . /
. . . But as I possess history, / I am possessed by it; it illuminates me: /
but what is the use of light?*]

A. Giuliani (in a piece written in 1957, now included in *Immagini e
maniere*, 1965, pp. 89-93) describes the metrics of this poetry as 'una
sorta di endecasillabo degenere, atonale, di stesura narrativa e arit-
mica' ['a sort of degenerate, toneless hendecasyllable of rhythmless
narrative design'] and suspects the subject-matter of being a mere
pretext for Pasolini's 'sensualità verbale'. This is true, and yet not the
truth. For the conscious, uneasy ambiguity – confusion even – is the
very heart of Pasolini's poetry, and to dismiss it is to miss the most
important innovation in Italian poetic discourse since that brought
about by Ungaretti and Montale, more than a quarter of a century
previously. Whatever one feels about the quality of individual poems
of Pasolini's, there is no doubt, first, that he made extended discourse
once again possible in Italian poetry and, second, that he did so by
involving poetry, desperately, with the real world, the 'external'
world, and its problems – something which a whole generation of
'committed' and 'neo-realist' poets failed to bring off. The Italian
panoramas that fill much of Pasolini's poetry, with their too exquisite
descriptive colour and pervasive, ambiguous sexuality, do not suc-
ceed as epic, but they form sweeping limbs of an unquenchable spate
of discourse, rich in different levels of terminology and linguistic and
metaphorical resourcefulness to the point of facility. Plethora,
perhaps; Pasolini's intellectual strength is not proportionate to his
verbosity or emotionalism, granted. Yet his 'sofferto esibizionismo',
truthful if only in the uncomfortable awareness of its own falsity, is
one of the few convincingly authentic things to have broken through

43

the impeccable form and the monstrous egotism of recent and not so recent Italian poetry. Pasolini's pretexts and his self-indulgence are so transparent as not to matter. He goes on and on, book after book, laying bare his obscure political conscience – for such is the gist of nearly all his poetry, apart from some finely rhetorical polemical or satirical invective, literary controversy and projects for future poems, narratives, plays or films.

Pasolini's poetry, then, is an emotional and ideological sorting-yard. It remains to a more resolute mind to turn the instrument he has created to more solid purpose. From the later 1960s, Pasolini also used poetry for the dramatic monologues inserted in the experimental novel *Teorema* (1968) or as the medium for his plays: nor is the dramatic 'voice' always a mere disguise for Pasolini's own. But if in these later works Pasolini adopts his new-found poetic discourse for the dramatic monologues of the tortured bourgeois soul, his Roman prose narratives of the 1950s offend literary propriety in the opposite sense, by resorting to crude dialect.

*Ragazzi di vita* (1955) consists of loosely linked stories about the juvenile delinquent fringe of the shanties and slums on the outskirts of Rome. The stories collected in *Alì dagli occhi azzurri* (1965) were written in the same years as *Ragazzi*, or a little later, and extend the panorama of that same subproletarian world of pimps and prostitutes, thieves and scroungers. Pasolini amply characterises this world in the long poem *La ricchezza* (in *La religione del nostro tempo*, 1961) as well as in his 'Appunti per un poema popolare' in *Alì* (pp. 89-102). Ferretti castigates this area of Pasolini's writing for its 'estetismo del lercio' ['aestheticism of the sordid'] and hastens over it with evident embarrassment, as a self-indulgence unworthy of a Marxist. Non-Marxist critics have tended to show equal distaste but usually pass it off as an aesthetically motivated rejection of a merely documentary realism, a realism relying on the direct transcription of raw dialect and yet not exempt from *estetismi* and sentimental and moralistic intrusions by the author.

Once again, all this is true, and yet not the truth. For all his patent faults, Pasolini has presented, with incontrovertible vigour and fidelity and courage, a social reality profoundly disconcerting both to the proletarian moralism of conventional Marxists and to what is ultimately the bourgeois moralism of conventional non-Marxists. The very fact that this delinquent world exists, with its squalor and its amoralism, and its total opposition to the working world, bespeaks a

44

critical failure of both political establishments – the Marxist and the non-Marxist.

But more than that – and this is what few critics can stomach – one senses that Pasolini's real solidarity is with this teeming 'low life', the non-working world, as against the despised working world. It is his outdated Romantic primitivism – which Pasolini readily and half-penitently confesses – that cannot be tolerated by Order.*

Pasolini counted some of the pieces of *Alì* as among the best he had done – 'La notte brava', 'Accattone', 'Mamma Roma', 'La ricotta' – and Anzoino agrees with him.‡ *Una vita violenta* (1959) is an edifying but unsuccessful attempt to transcend this immemorial 'low life': Pasolini tries to make a novel, complete with central character, Tommaso Puzzilli, who progresses 'positively' from total unawareness to Fascist thuggery and then to Communism and the – to Pasolini – *petit bourgeois* dream of marriage, home and respectability. 'Accattone' and 'Mamma Roma' (which Pasolini filmed in uncompromising dialect) show 'society' as a world out of reach of the respective protagonists, who are pulled back irresistibly into their gutter. The ever-present risk of death, or the near-death of prison, lends a baroque drama to their lives. Mamma Roma's despairing tirade on the inescapable heredity of her kind ends with the unanswerable and all too answerable: 'E allora, de chi è la colpa? La responsabbilità?' [Well then, whose fault is it? Who's responsible?'], to which the author's literary response is the image of the dirty scrap of paper carried along the road and left there by the sea wind (*Alì dagli occhi azzurri*, pp. 436-7). The pathos of this contrasts with the pathos, in 'Accattone', of the virginal Stella finally consenting to whore for the upkeep of her abominable lover – and finding herself, in the event, unable to go through with it. Then 'La notte brava' renders the dizzy wheeling of fortune with a fantastic, deadly gaiety unknown to the complacent Boccaccio, while social fatality is most inexorably worked out in 'Mignotta'.

The charge of irresponsible, self-indulgent irrationalism forms the refrain of criticism of Pasolini. But what he presents, in various guises, is *pre-rational*: that is, a reality that Reason has failed to deal with or has simply ignored. To go on ignoring it – that is indeed irrational. The pre-rational in Pasolini's Roman works is the gaiety, viciousness and pointlessness of the life of those who lack an 'honest'

---

*See T. Anzoino, Pasolini, *p. 44.*
‡*See O. Stack, Pasolini on Pasolini: Interviews with Oswald Stack, *p. 31; and Anzoino,* Pasolini, *p. 56.*

livelihood or refuse to be serfs to those who 'perché ciànno un po' de grana in saccoccia se credono chissà che sono!' (*Alí*, p. 425) ['just because they've got some money in their pockets take themselves for God knows who!']. In *Teorema* (1968) and the verse-plays, the pre-rational wreaks its vengeance on the bourgeois world that has reduced everything to a semblance of rationality. In the guise of the male genitalia, the pre-rational destroys that flimsy conventional world: the stranger in *Teorema* (also a film) who ravishes maidservant, son, daughter, mother and father; in *Affabulazione* (published in 1969 in *Nuovi argomenti*, no. 15, pp. 14-112), the father's curiosity and loving envy of his son's sexuality, most explicitly enacted, ending with son stabbing father with a knife – given by the father – that represents that sexuality. In each work, *la ragione* is Pasolini's target, in opposition to his notion of *religione contadina* in *Teorema* and sexuality as *mistero* in *Affabulazione*. Ideologically, Pasolini makes the banal error of confusing the false rationality of the bourgeois-communist world diarchy with 'Reason' as such. (We might also mention his repeated invectives against the youthful *contestazione* as a new Nazism, which compounds this confusion.) Artistically, his high bourgeois tragedy is transparently contrived and pretentious. He flounders, and his vaunted *canone sospeso* ['open canon'] is no excuse. Yet the potency of his writing and of his imagination – both in overall design and in the details – survives the frequently frightful lapses and ramblings of his verse.

Pasolini's main interest was to turn to the *cinema di poesia*. On the whole, his literary work produced foundations rather than edifices. It remains to be seen whether some other writer will build further on those foundations.

## Calvino's macrocosm: the politics of play

> Only laughter can offer us a revolutionary mutation of human consciousness.

With these words Calvino ends his brief 'Considerations on Sex and Laughter' (in *20th-Century Studies*, 2, November 1969, pp. 103-5). Yet Calvino's narrative fiction never echoes the belly-laugh of an Aristophanes or a Rabelais. Nor does he learn from the subversive fantasies of Lewis Carroll's *Alice* books, though he admires them. Ariosto's genteel irony and humour and R. L. Stevenson's spirit of adventure have left a greater mark on Calvino's writing and help to define its limits.

His literary thumbprint is clearly distinguishable right from the start in his first book, *Il sentiero dei nidi di ragno* (1947), and has remained essentially unchanged since then. Perhaps what strikes us first is the adolescent viewpoint of the narrative. The boy protagonist, Pin, knows everything – that men fornicate and kill – but understands nothing. Elsewhere, the age may vary: Quinto Anfossi in *La speculazione edilizia* (1957) and Amerigo Ormea in *La giornata di uno scrutatore* (1963) are youngish men; Qfwfq in *Le cosmicomiche* (1965) and *Ti con zero* (1967) has been an ageless adolescent since before the beginning of the universe or of time itself, though he is introduced as 'il vecchio Qfwfq'; Marco Polo and Kublai Kan in *Le città invisibili* (1972) inhabit a continuum from young manhood to middle age. All Calvino's protagonists are mystified by the world in which they live. This incomprehension of the world appears so regularly in Calvino's narrative works that it comes over as autobiographical – a baffled rationalism which is Calvino's central limitation. He is non-plussed and therefore non-committal – quite the opposite to Lewis Carroll's Alice, the wise child who *sees through* the vicious sham of the adult world.

The author's thumbprint in *Il sentiero* shows other features which will recur throughout his work. Two are complementary: a sensory curiosity and a Euclidean geometry. Calvino's curious pen pokes at the amorphous miscellany of the sensory world, natural, human and man-made, dwelling especially on the stickily tactile and visually grotesque: the warty faces of the tatterdemalion partisan band; Pin's spiders' nests and the shiny P-38 pistol he has stolen, almost magical in its self-contained power; misty forests. In subsequent works, Calvino's descriptive curiosity frequently coagulates in his distinctive long panoramic sentences, which sometimes extend for a page or more, taking in a whole harbourful of folk, or a ski-run, a bustling landscape or the whole universe of signs, a great city full of soap-bubbles or the moon's curd-like coating – every detail noted with elegant precision.

Calvino's geometrical ingenuity often leads him to similar syntactic *tours de force*. Its main appearance in *Il sentiero* is Lupo Rosso's theorem-like account of his shooting of the traitor Pelle. In *La giornata*, the pseudo-Hegelian dilemmas of the election-scrutineer are traced out in long-limbed sentences as a sort of mental geometry, and there is a famous triangular perspective, involving Ormea, a politician and a dwarf in the Cottolengo institution. A great number of Calvino's shorter narratives hinge on symmetries or asymmetries, inversion, circularity, tangents, parallels, and so on. In stories such as 'Giochi senza fine' (in *Le cosmicomiche*), Calvino plays with at least some notions of post-Einsteinian geometry, while *Ti con zero* is explicitly mathematical both in its title and discourse, and the most recently published *Le città invisibili* and *Il castello dei destini incrociati* (1973) are colourful exercises in structuralist semiology.

Fantasy is the component that completes and subsumes Calvino's literary personality. *Il sentiero*, apparently concerned with the political and historical reality of the Resistance struggle, has always been seen as a woodland fable. Even the more starkly documentary works – *La speculazione edilizia*, *La giornata di uno scrutatore*, 'La nuvola di smog' (1958) – give extensive scope to both the jackdaw curiosity and the abstract geometry, while his urban short stories in *Gli amori difficili* (most of which are included, along with 'La nuvola di smog', in the *Racconti* collection of 1958 and were re-published with the same story as a separate volume in 1970) and *Marcovaldo, ovvero le stagioni in città* (1963) constitute a strong argument for the claim that Calvino's essential talent lies in presenting reality as fantasy. Fantasy becomes the very stuff of the rest of Calvino's work: we have the historical fantasies indicated in the very titles of the trilogy *Il visconte dimezzato* (1951), *Il barone rampante* (1957) and *Il cavaliere inesistente* (1959), published collectively as *I nostri antenati* (1960) with an interesting preface. The short stories of *Le cosmicomiche* and *Ti con zero* turn to cosmic fantasy and (in the latter) to genetics, cybernetics, mathematics and narrative composition itself as vehicles of fantasy. *Le città invisibili* and *Il castello* are semiological fantasies elaborated through Marco Polo's portraits of fifty-five cities and the Tarot cards respectively.

All these features – laughter, bafflement, sensory curiosity, geometrical games and fantasy – add up to a kind of writing that is *play* in a more specific sense than that in which all art is play. Play, for Calvino, is largely the matter, as well as the manner, of his writing. In other words, not only is writing a form of play for him, but it describes play and adventure. Play is indeed the central political issue of Calvino's writing, as it is its central aesthetic issue. It is more politically significant – at least in the long run – than the surface political issues of Calvino's titles: issues such as property speculation, electoral manipulation, atmospheric pollution, urban claustrophobia. The play-element is also more politically significant than the explicitly political themes that crop up in the historical trilogy – the debunking of militarism, institutional man and feudalism; the social upheaval of the French Revolution, and so on (even given the relevance of these themes to the recent experience of Fascist Italy).

Communist critics, in fact, were blinkering themselves when, in the 1950s, they deplored the 'escapist' element in Calvino, himself a Resistance fighter and a member of the Italian Communist Party until he left it in 1957 in the aftermath of the Hungarian tragedy. J. R. Woodhouse and others have ably shown how Calvino's narrative fantasies of the 1950s are no less concerned than the literature of *neorealismo* with serious political issues: primarily, with the general alienation of society, but, more specifically, with the class system, the defacement of the human and natural environment, bureaucracy and authoritarianism, the involution and misdirection of science and culture. Calvino's tirelessly inventive narrative work is full of such concerns. Yet, to restrict attention to these concerns is to risk fragmenting Calvino as a writer. He stands or falls, politically and artistically, by the potency of his play.

Despite my opening quotation, Calvino's play is limited in its potency. In keeping with the whole tradition of Italian literature, Calvino adheres strictly to what one might call a 'closed aesthetic', as opposed to the 'open aesthetic' of an Aristophanes, a Rabelais or a Shakespeare. By this I mean that each of his narratives works within rigid co-ordinates of both form and content (the two, of course, defining one another). The author himself has often declared that his method of writing is to work out an initial idea or image in all its interesting possibilities. Thus, the danger which Calvino always courts is that of being trapped in a formal exercise. An open aesthetic, by contrast, would be one in which the formal and thematic premises are transcended. In his longer narratives, such as those of the trilogy, Calvino stays with his initial idea too long. In *Il cavaliere inesistente*, for example, it seems to be the armour that wins the day. True, Torrismondo hangs his up, to join the liberated Curvaldians as an equal. True also, the non-existent Agilulfo comes to an amusing end. But the typically bemused protagonist, Rambaldo, inherits Agilulfo's armour without apparently having transcended its inexorable logic. Similarly, in *Il barone rampante*, Cosimo remains trapped in his tree-top individualism, to die, after all, defeated – though it does not emerge very clearly that he *is* defeated, or why, and this inconclusiveness is the main weakness of Calvino's narrative and ideological enterprise. This

49

is a pity in a story which begins by escaping the confines of class society and healing both the breach between work and play and that between history and nature. The most striking instance of opaqueness is *Le città invisibili*. The title's warning of opaqueness does not excuse it. For Calvino's choice of Marco Polo and Kublai Kan as his protagonists implies Money and Power as two ways of 'knowing' the world. Yet, in rendering the two men's sense of failure to know their invisible female cities, Calvino never looks at them 'through' Power or Money and poses the problematic abstractly, and prematurely, as one of language, and perhaps of existence itself.

Calvino's play, then, is limited in its cognitive and subversive potential, because in each narrative the writer sticks strictly to an initial set of rules. He is, as it were, programmed. He himself is the adolescent unable or unwilling to transcend the data provided by traditional or modern culture and society. Bolder play, blurring or kaleidoscopically rearranging or insolently crystallising (as does Brecht) conventional ways of seeing the world, could have opened out to Calvino the richest opportunities available to recent Italian writing. Nevertheless, his achievements are diverse and considerable, and he has given us some of the most variously delightful and compelling writing in modern Italian. In *Gli amori difficili* Calvino's play comes most closely to grips with the world we live in and its everyday tension between Eros and Alienation. *Marcovaldo* shows that same world with its inescapable humble disappointments forever springing into ingenuous, colourful fantasy and adventure, like the children's soap-bubbles, conjured out of nothing (or out of free detergent samples) and evaporating into nothing. The fantastic trilogy follows human endeavour into history and nature. Calvino's later experiments with pseudo-scientific fantasy are on the whole not so sustained in their purpose, though he is always capable of bringing off an unforgettable descriptive or dialectic *tour de force*. Yet the cosmic and genetic saga that grows out of *Le cosmicomiche* and *Ti con zero*, from the first nebulae to the skyscrapers of New York, and from the first living cells to modern cybernetic codes, is an imposing theme most ingeniously cast into narrative form with plenty of suspense and surprises. The attempts, in *La città invisibili* and *Il castello dei destini incrociati*, to make a semiological drama of the process of communication and of artistic composition itself, with the various kinds of despair implied, are nobly self-defeating – an obsession that Calvino himself hopes that he has succeeded in exorcising.

Calvino's political *and* literary task is to try to regain control of his play, which he lost before he had properly found it, in the confusion ensuing from his loss of faith in Communism and his failure to find a satisfactory alternative perspective to prop up his intense need for optimism.

## Terruggi's monster

Inauthenticity is both the matter and the manner of Terruggi's trick novel, *Luisa e il Presidente* (Rome, Edizioni Mediterranee, 1972). The ambiguous elegance of the writing, its cool and ghastly control, manage to equate *cliché* and *tour de force* (the two extremes of stylistic inauthenticity) with a combination of understatement, suspense, false solutions, incongruity, farce, casual but devastating surprises, sudden shifts and reversals and breath-taking anti-climax, that holds the reader's attention through all the book's bewildering inconsequentialities and incomprehensible horrors. Terruggi wrests words and moulds sentences out of a semantic and existential void with sustained yet unassuming brilliance. The slightest raising of tone, an unexpected adjective, produce an unbearable tension. The low tone is at once bureaucratic and classical – that is, rooted in the inauthentic heart of Italian linguistic culture. It describes minutely and concretely, but with detachment and poise. The destruction of a whole fleet in a typhoon (pp. 123-4), narrated in perfectly rounded periods, gains rather than loses in horror from this simultaneity of immediacy and aloofness.

The typhoon episode is written in the narrative past. The rest is in a weirdly conjectural present, a first-person diary kept by Silvio, who has lost his sense of time and has been working for seven, or possibly thirteen, years in the labyrinthine offices of the mysterious and sinister SALS (Società Anonima Libera Segreta). Silvio may have been the sole survivor of the typhoon disaster (' . . . possiamo dubitare che chi ha visto l'occhio del tifone non acquisisca capacità intellettuali e facoltà di intuizione molto al di sopra della norma?', p. 132 ['can we doubt that someone who has looked into the eye of the typhoon must acquire intellectual abilities and faculties of intuition far above the norm?']) and seems to be writing both before and after the event in the *same* employee capacity. Yet the survivor has had his entire personality taken away and replaced with a plastic one, though he has outwit-

51

ted the system (SALS) by pretending that the shock 'therapy' he has been given has completely erased his memory of the disaster.

Other figures in the book seem to have multiple identities or to slide temporarily into anonymity. For example, the Press Officer (or secret police chief?), Serpioni, can be recognised as the high Admiralty official who presides benignly over the survivor's obliteration, by his friendly-Judas way of clasping his victim just above the elbows, but is also described in the same words as the odious man who forcibly buys up every painting of Guido's before the public can see it.

We are in a literary nightmare which is the counterpart to the 'one-dimensional' technological society in which class-struggle does not exist and the workers have become obedient and anonymous automata: the *commessi* who guard the innumerable corridors and lifts of the SALS building (which extends its tentacular control, perhaps, over the whole necropolis – as Silvio cannot help pronouncing 'metropolis') – and the jovial overalled men who carry out the SALS's sinister strong-arm work. It is an indecipherable, labyrinthine *1984*.

Terruggi (who works for the Italian Parliament) plays on the fact that in Italian *Consiglio* can mean both 'Company Board' and 'Ministerial Cabinet'; *Presidente* both 'Company Chairman' and 'Prime Minister' or 'Head of State'; *Società*, both 'Company' and 'social system' or 'society' in general. He also offers interpretative bait at several political levels of *cliché* and *tour de force* – all quite inconclusive, even when all seems on the point of being resolved, as when Silvio at last meets the hitherto inaccessible President or when he decides to marry Luisa.

Political and existential bait are cunningly mixed. The book opens with the monster: a leering face which appears to Silvio for a split second when he least expects it. Silvio sees its image in Guido's painting (chapter 9) and then finds it repeated in all Guido's paintings that the SALS has hidden away in an obscure basement (chapter 15). Finally he decides to marry Luisa and tame the monster, by living with it: 'Sarò tutt'uno col mostro' (p. 202) ['I shall be one with the monster'].

Then there are Luisa's creeping paralysis and the mysterious complaints which affect all the men except Silvio and the *commessi* and *uomini in tuta*. There is the fact that nearly everybody is faceless, 'irriconoscibile' to Silvio. There is psychological bait: it could all be Silvio's schizoid fantasy. Terruggi clearly knows what literature cannot legitimately do but all too often illegitimately foists on the reader.

52

He is aware of the passing off of social or political assumptions, prejudices, injunctions, as metaphysical axioms or neutral, 'objective' data. He is aware of the aesthetic arrogance which sets itself up as transcendance of the world we live in. He is aware, like Vittorini, of 'l'autoritarismo dello scrittore che si crede Dio' ['the authoritarianism of the writer who takes himself for God'] and that literature is impotent politically, an idle and lonely game – except in so far as it possesses a 'potere conoscitivo' ['cognitive power'], even if this reveals itself, in Terruggi, as the impossibility of knowing anything through the conventions of mere 'literature'. For to say that nothing *can* be known is itself a political presumption and an alibi, and inauthenticity involves literature no less than the world of which literature is a product. In *Luisa e il Presidente*, unpretentiously, but firmly, knowingly, literature stares itself in its blind eye.

*Chapter Three*

# Recapitulation

The writers I have discussed may not be statistically significant – even if literary history lends itself to statistical treatment. However, they are indicative of the political issues that have dominated post-war literature in Italy.

The Marxian impetus has been central, though often vague. The Italian Communist Party tried to hold the allegiance of writers in a broad cultural movement during the 1940s and 1950s under the banner of 'realism', while in the 1960s the impetus of the Left carried on even more vaguely under that of 'alienation'. The PCI, in its effort to hold the mass of both the intellectuals and the people, encouraged the blurring of theory, whether regarding society, politics, economics or literature itself, burying the crucial notions of class struggle and the workers' revolution in an amorphous populism and humanitarianism with the Soviet Union as exemplar.

Betti and Montale had already reacted against this perspective: seeing in it a materialist collectivism, they counterpose a transcendental individualism. Guareschi – the only true Italian populist (even in style) of the nine writers – achieves the Catholic-Communist amalgam, reflecting the new Italy, its material satisfaction and its mental confusion. The other writers, shading from rationalist progressive to visionary utopian, explore, refine or transcend various aspects of the vague populist realism which was the general cultural starting-point. Silone defines *popolo* precisely as the peasantry and realism as the intellectual's identification with the peasantry and focuses on their class exploitation and the key political problem of ending (not just changing) it. Lampedusa transcends conventional realism by his new combination of a broad social and historical perspective with a microscopic view of a politically strategic individual, using a style to match that individual's sensibility and culture. Pavese's autobiographical individualism concentrates on the literarily trained intellectual himself, unable to make the transition from uncommitted aesthete to social and political being, with sexual betrayal as the most dramatic area in which the failure operates. Pasolini also sees the problem of politics as rooted in sexuality: but instead of presenting the individual as his own victim, like Pavese (or Betti), he deliberately scandalises the prim and repressive society, whether capitalist or Leninist, and thus characterises social groups (rather like Lawrence) in erotic as well as class terms.

Calvino's way of breaking out of flat realism is through fantasy and play, concentrating especially on sensory reality and on mental constructs: he thus implicitly dismisses the notion of humanitarian populism in favour of human reason or science but eventually falls prey to abstractness in the process. Terruggi, inheriting the experiments of the 1960s, is far removed from wishful notions of realism and populism and uses a disciplined surrealistic technique to demolish the modern world's pretensions to 'reality'. So, over and above explicitly political themes, religion, sex, conventions of knowledge and reality, style, language and literature itself are explored by these writers in their political implications. All of them turn what at first sight may seem to be a non-political concern into an explicitly political concern. They make connections between politics and 'life in general'.

Where, then, do Italian writers leave us in the face of the problems of the world today – problems which are *also* political problems? Two or three negative things stand out clearly. Italian literature at this moment has quite lost the old Christian convictions, which it used to have, that sexuality is sin and that salvation is a lonely, ascetic, transcendental business. Indeed, Christian convictions seem altogether to have gone out of literature, and even a metaphysically inclined poet such as Mario Luzi has latterly turned towards a more dubitative poetry which is correspondingly more open to a dialogue with the poet's fellow human beings. Equally, however, confidence in achieving terrestrial solutions has disappeared. Resistance and revolution, people and Party have led only to a dubious consumer society which is all-pervasive despite its unconcealable deformities. Most important of all, the residual faith in literature itself as a superior, redeeming activity has buried itself in its inevitable resting-place – a closed aesthetic implying one sort or another of despairing or complacent determinism. All these defeats seem related to the failure of literature to break outside the cultured class (though, to be sure, that class has been extended), which, in turn, is related to the failure of Italian society, in common with probably the whole of modern society, to become truly one. At the same time, this loss of confidence in literature marks the coming of age of Italy's urban industrial society, its final shift from the quasi-caste system of a predominantly agrarian and settled society.

This leaves literature, for the time being, with only one role – that of critique. And, as we have seen, the nine writers we have studied are valuable precisely for the quality and originality of their critique. Disappointment heightens awareness, including political awareness. Whereas, in the past, writers acquired a too exclusively literary training, they now realise that this is not enough. An understanding of political, economic and social structures, of historical processes, of psychological and sexual relationships is now seen as a necessary reinforcement of pure intuition, which Croce's vast influence had all but established as the sole principle of aesthetics; while the conventions of realism have been replaced by a whole range of imaginative tools (including forms of ultra-realism) for penetrating, dismantling and rearranging the world we live in. The arid and destructive theoretical debates of the 1960s have burnt out many naiveties. All this is giving Italy an ever more experimental literature which is certainly by no means free of gimmickry but whose potential is already easily discernible in the writers we have examined. In this, too, Italy's is not radically different from most other literatures. And some positives are visible – in various forms, a new vitalism different from that more simple vitalism of the Resistance. There is the Eros, though too confused, of Pasolini. There is the play, as yet not ebullient or impudent enough, of Calvino. Other forms of vitalism that have not yet matured can be made out vaguely. This need not mean – indeed, *cannot* mean – a facile nineteenth-century optimism. Our world is too terrifying for that. It can mean that literature has the opportunity to offer us livable perspectives: things for which it is acceptable to live and – which is synonymous – ways in which it is acceptable for us all to live together. These are grand political subjects for literature. They are worth holding out against the ever-recurring temptation for literature to make itself the Idol.

# Notes

*The bibliographical information given below is intended for guidance only and is in no sense exhaustive. Even in the Notes for Chapter Two no attempt has been made to list all the publications of any individual author or the full editorial history of single works.*

*Introduction:* The Literature of Politics and the Politics of Literature in Italy

Dante's politics are discussed in J. Goudet's *Dante et la politique* (Aubier, Paris, 1969). There is an interesting review of Goudet's book by R. Tessari, 'Attualità della dimensione ideologica reazionaria nella poesia', in *Lettere italiane*, XXII, 1970 (pp. 399-405). See also 'La polemica su Dante: ovvero un esempio di politica culturale del PCI', in *Movimento Studentesco*, January 1974.

An initial discussion on the autonomy or otherwise of the individual can be found in E. H. Carr, *What is History?* (Macmillan, London, 1961, and Penguin, Harmondsworth, 1964, 1970[5]), Ch. 2: 'Society and the Individual'; and in Peter L. Berger, *Invitation to Sociology* (Doubleday, New York, 1963, and Penguin, Harmondsworth, 1966, 1976), Ch. 5: 'Society in Man'.

Two books on the cultured class in Italy are: Strappini/Micocci/Abruzzese, *La classe dei colti. Intellettuali e società nel primo Novecento italiano* (Laterza, Bari, 1970), and, outstandingly interesting, S. Piccone-Stella, *Intellettuali e capitale nella società italiana del dopoguerra* (De Donato, Bari, 1972). On the social and political implications of the levels of literacy, see: C. M. Cipolla, *Literacy and the Development of the West* (Penguin, Harmondsworth, 1969).

*Chapter One:* People and Politics in Post-war Italy

Invaluable on all main aspects of Italy's emergence from Fascism is *The Rebirth of Italy: 1943-1950*, ed. S. J. Woolf (Longman, London, 1972). Luigi Cortesi's 'I quarantacinque giorni', serialised in *L'Espresso*, Rome, from 29 July to 9 September 1973, is a detailed account of Italian politics from the fall of Mussolini to Badoglio's armistice with the USA, the USSR and Britain. R. Zangrandi covers the same ground in *1943: 25 luglio – 8 settembre* (Feltrinelli, Milan, 1964). The armistice itself is analysed by R. Zangrandi in *L'Italia tradita: 8-9-1943* (Mursia, Milan, 1971). For an introduction to the Marxist problematic of revolution as it relates to post-Fascist Italy, see S. Avineri, *The Social and Political Thought of Karl Marx* (Cambridge University Press, 1968), Ch. 6: 'The Revolutionary Dialectics of Capitalist Society'.

On the Italian Resistance see: R. Battaglia, *Storia della Resistenza italiana* (Einaudi, Turin, 1953); G. Quazza, *La Resistenza italiana* (1966); and G. Bocca, *Storia dell'Italia partigiana* (Laterza, Bari, 1967).

Italy's history since the war is concisely discussed by E. Wiskemann in her *Italy since 1945* (Macmillan, London, 1971), and more extensively in: M. Grindrod, *The Rebuilding of Italy: 1945-1955* (Royal Institute of International Affairs, London and New York, 1955) and also her *Italy* (Benn, London, 1968); M. Carlyle, *Modern Italy* (Hutchinson, London, 1957; revised edition 1965); P. A. Allum, *Italy – Republic without Government?* (Weidenfeld and Nicolson, London, 1973) and *The Italian Communist Party since 1945: grandeurs and servitudes of a European socialist strategy* (University of Reading Graduate School of Contemporary European Studies, 1970). On the problems of the South and of agriculture, see: M. Rossi-Doria, *Dieci anni di politica agraria nel Mezzogiorno* (Laterza, Bari, 1958); M. Carlyle, *The Awakening of Southern Italy* (Oxford University Press, London, 1962); *Rural Social Development* (Report of a UN European Study Group on Rural Social Development in the Framework of Development in Southern Italy, held at Naples and Metaponto in 1965, published by L'Amministrazione per le Attività Assistenziali Italiane e Internazionali, Rome, July 1965); S. H. Franklin, *The European Peasantry: The Final Phase* (Methuen, London, 1969), Ch. 4: '*Contadini*: Peasant and Capitalist Farming in the Mezzogiorno'; C. Barberis, *Gli operai-contadini: sociologia del Piano Mansholt* (Il Mulino, Bologna, 1970) and 'Men, Farms and Product in Italian Agriculture', in *Review of the Economic Conditions in Italy*, Banco di Roma, XXV/5, September 1971; G. Marselli, *La civiltà contadina e la trasformazione delle campagne* (Loescher, Turin, 1973); and P. Villani, *Mezzogiorno tra riforme e rivoluzione* (Laterza, Bari, 1973).

The handbook on the role of the Catholic Church in Italian politics is A. A. Jemolo, *Chiesa e Stato in Italia dall'Unificazione a Giovanni XXIII* (Einaudi, Turin, 1965). See also C. Pallenberg, *Vatican*

*Finances* (Peter Owen, London, 1971). Specifically on the post-war Church, see: G. De Rosa, S.I., *Cattolici e comunisti oggi in Italia* ('La civiltà cattolica', Rome, 1966), and A. D'Alfonso (ed.), *I Cattolici e il Dissenso* (Editori Riuniti, Rome, 1969).

Fascist-type conspiracies to take over the country were discovered in 1967, in December 1970 and November 1973. The worst bomb outrages were the seven train bombs of 8 August 1969 and the notorious massacre at Piazza Fontana, in Milan, on 12 December 1969, but from 1969 there was a steady sequence of assassinations of potential court witnesses and of attacks on Communist and Socialist branch offices and on synagogues, and in May, 1974, the worst bomb massacre of all, in a crowded square in Brescia. Since then anarchist and revolutionary groups of the left have been increasingly active in kidnappings and also some killings, while in 1976 right-wing terrorists were assassinating magistrates opposed to them at the rate of one a week.

*Towards the suicide of literature?*
The political attitudes of Italian writers this century have received considerable attention. Critical assessment of individual authors almost invariably includes or implies political and ideological analysis. By way of introduction, see: Strappini/Micocci/Abruzzese, *La classe dei colti (cit.);* M. Isenghi, *Il mito della Grande Guerra* (Laterza, Bari, 1969); A. Asor Rosa, *Scrittori e popolo* (Samonà e Savelli, Rome, 1971(2)); G. F. Venè, *Letteratura e capitalismo in Italia dal '700 a oggi* (Sugar, Milan, 1963) and *Pirandello fascista* (1971): both these titles are now available in one paperback volume, *Capitale e letteratura* (Garzanti, Milan, 1974); A. Hamilton, *The Appeal of Fascism: A Study of Intellectuals and Fascism, 1919-1945* (Blond, London, 1973); N. Bobbio, 'Cultura e costume fra il '35 e il '40', in P. Alatri *et al., Trent'anni di storia politica italiana* (ERI, Turin, 1967), pp. 359-72; E. R. Tannenbaum, *Fascism in Italy: Society and Culture 1922-1945* (Allen Lane, London, 1973); G. Quazza, *Fascismo e società italiana* (Einaudi, Turin, 1973); E. A. Albertoni, E. Antonini, R. Palmieri (eds.), *La generazione degli anni difficili* (Laterza, Bari, 1962); G. Cattaneo, *Letteratura e ribellione* (Rizzoli, Milan, 1972); and S. Piccone-Stella, *Intellettuali e capitale (cit.)*; Nello Ajello, *Lo scrittore e il potere* (Laterza, Bari, 1974). General works on post-war Italian literature are: E. Falqui, *Novecento letterario* (Vallecchi, Florence, 10 vols., 1954-69, re-published in 6 vols., from 1970); G. Manacorda,

*Letteratura italiana contemporanea (1940-1965)* (Editori Riuniti, Rome, 1967); G. Bárberi Squarotti, *La narrativa italiana del dopoguerra* (Cappelli, Bologna, 1965) and *La cultura e la poesia italiana del dopoguerra* (Cappelli, Bologna, 1966); D. Fernandez, *Il romanzo italiano e la crisi della coscienza moderna* (Lerici, Milan, 1960). Also useful are E. Cecchi and N. Sapegno (eds.), *Storia della letteratura italiana*, vol. IX, *Il Novecento* (Garzanti, Milan, 1969); and the studies of individual authors by various scholars contained in *Orientamenti Culturali: Letteratura italiana – I Contemporanei* (3 vols, Marzorati, Milan, 1963 and 1969) and in the series 'Il Castoro', published by La Nuova Italia, Florence, and still in progress.

*Neorealismo* is briefly discussed in G. Manacorda, *op.cit.*, pp. 28-36 (see esp. p. 33). See also: Frank Rosengarten, 'The Italian Resistance Novel (1945-1962)', in *From 'Verismo' to Experimentalism: Essays on the Modern Italian Novel*, ed. S. Pacifici (Indiana University Press, 1969), pp. 212-38 and 279; and Bruce Merry, 'The Italian partisan novel: theme and variations', *Mediterranean Review*, 2, n. 4 (1972), pp. 68-75.

Gramsci's 'Quaderni del carcere' were published after his death in six volumes by Einaudi between 1948 and 1951. Those most relevant here are *Il materialismo storico e la filosofia di Benedetto Croce* and *Gli intellettuali e l'organizzazione della cultura* (both of 1948) and *Letteratura e vita nazionale* (1950). Einaudi have since brought out a critical edition of 'Quaderni del carcere' by V. Gerretana, in 4 vols., in 1975, and Gramsci's complete *Opere* in 12 vols. (1954-71). On Gramsci, see: S. Piccone-Stella, *op.cit.*, pp. 79-86; and N. Stipcević, *Gramsci e i problemi letterari* (Mursia, Milan, 1968). A classic discussion of this whole area is A. Asor Rosa, *op.cit.*, 'La Resistenza e il gramscianesimo: apogeo e crisi del populismo', pp. 189-348. Some of Gramsci's writings have been published in English by Lawrence and Wishart, London, in *The Modern Prince and other writings* (1957) and *Selections from the Prison Notebooks* (1971).

On Vittorini's role in *Il Politecnico* and his controversy with Togliatti, see M. Zancan, ' "Il Politecnico" e il PCI tra Resistenza e dopoguerra', in *Il Ponte*, XXIX, 7-8 (July-August, 1973: a special number dedicated to Vittorini), pp. 994-1010. Vittorini's *Diario in pubblico* (Bompiani, Milan 1970²) and *Le due tensioni: appunti per un'ideologia della letteratura* (Il Saggiatore, Milan, 1967) centre on the political responsibilities of literature.

The literary debates of the post-war period, including those of the *avant-garde* of the 1960s, are generously documented in Manacorda's book. See also *20th-century Studies*, 5 (September 1971), dedicated to essays by prominent Italian writers on *Culture and Ideology in Post-War Italy*. The literature market is analysed by E. Sanguineti, 'Sopra l'avanguardia' (1963), now in *Ideologia e linguaggio* (Feltrinelli, Milan, 1965), pp. 54-8, and also in the *TLS* number on *Money in Literature* (25 September 1969). There is an anthology, *Avanguardia e neoavanguardia* (Sugar, Milan, 1966), with an introduction by G. Ferrata.

*Chapter Two:* Nine Writers

*Ugo Betti: the whore as queen*

Nearly all Betti's plays are published in *Teatro completo* (1957), by Cappelli, Bologna, who have also published his poems and narrative works. His 1914 thesis, 'Il diritto e la rivoluzione', is included in *Scritti inediti* (Edizioni del Centro Librario, Bari, 1964), ed. A. di Pietro. *Religione e teatro*, written in 1953, was published in 1957. An English version appeared in *Tulane Drama Review* V, No. 2 (December 1960), pp. 3-12. The same journal, VIII, No. 3 (Spring 1964) carried a selection of *Essays, Correspondence, Notes* by Betti (pp. 51-86). G. H. McWilliam has translated *Three Plays on Justice* by Betti (Chandler, San Francisco, 1964), and Henry Reed has translated *The Queen and the Rebels, The Burnt Flower-Bed* and *Summertime (Il Paese delle vacanze)* in *Three Plays* (Gollancz, London, 1956), and *Crime on Goat Island* (Samuel French, London, 1960).

The most useful books on Betti are: F. Cologni, *U.B.* (Cappelli, Bologna, 1960), and G. Moro, *Il teatro di U.B.* (Marzorati, Milan, 1973). Good essays or chapters on Betti are: J. A. Scott, 'The Message of U.B.', in *Italica*, XXXVII, 1960, pp. 44-57; G. H. McWilliam, 'Interpreting Betti', *Tulane Drama Review*, V, No. 2 (December 1960), pp. 15-23, and 'The minor plays of U.B.', in *Italian Studies*, XX (1965), pp. 78-107; also his introduction to *Two Plays* by Betti (Manchester University Press, 1965); G. Rizzo, 'Regression-Progression in U.B.'s Drama', in *Tulane Drama Review*, VIII, No. 1 (Fall 1963), pp. 101-29; G. Pullini, in *Cinquant'anni di teatro in Italia* (Cappelli, Rocca San Casciano, 1960), pp. 85-93; Vito Pandolfi, 'Italian Theatre Since the War', in *Tulane Drama Review*, VIII, No. 3 (Spring 1964), pp. 87-107 (pp. 92-4 are on Betti); and G. Genot, 'U.B.: l'engrenage et la balance', in P. Brunel (ed.), *La mort de Godot: attente et évanescence au théatre* ('Lettres Modernes', Minard, Paris, 1970), pp. 75-112.

*Manichee and hierophant: Montale's negative epiphany*

Montale is receiving more and more critical attention. The fullest study of his poetry is M. Forti, *Eugenio Montale: la poesia, la prosa di fantasia e d'invenzione* (Mursia, Milan, 1973). On the post-war Montale, see: U. Carpi, *Montale dopo il fascismo: dalla 'Bufera' a 'Satura'* (Liviana, Padua, 1971), particularly attentive to Montale's political ideology; O. Macrí, 'Esegesi del terzo libro di Montale', in *Realtà del Simbolo* (Vallecchi, Florence, 1968), pp. 73-146; Costanzo di Girolamo, 'Appunti per l'ultimo Montale', in *Belfagor*, XXVII/3 (31/5/1973), pp. 350-63; G. Zagarrio, 'Poesia settanta e il "sistema" – L'ostinazione del "sopravvivere" in Montale', in *Il Ponte*, XXIX, No. 1, 31/1/1973, pp. 83-97. The journals *Letteratura* and *La Rassegna della letteratura italiana* each devoted a whole number to Montale in 1966. G. Nascimbeni, *Eugenio Montale* (Longanesi, Milan, 1969) is a useful biography. There are full-length studies in English by G. Singh (Yale University Press, 1973); Joseph Cary, in *Three Modern Italian Poets* (New York University Press, 1969); and G. Almansi and B. Merry, *M.* (Edinburgh University Press, 1977). See also: F. J. Jones, 'Montale's Dialectic of Memory', in *Italian Studies*, Vol. XXVIII (1973), pp. 83-107 and the same author's *La poesia italiana contemporania da Gozzano a Quasimodo* (D'Anna, Messina, 1976).

Montale's works are published by Mondadori, unless otherwise stated. Crucial to an understanding of the poet is his self-exegesis, 'Intenzioni – intervista immaginaria' (despite its title, mainly retrospective), first published in 1946, and since in G. Spagnoletti (ed.), *Poesia italiana contemporanea (1909-1959)* (Guanda, Parma, 1959), pp. 341-8. A selection of Montale's poems is available in English (Edinburgh University Press, 1964, and Penguin, Harmondsworth, 1969).

*Giuseppe Tomasi Di Lampedusa's*
Il Gattopardo: *the owl of Minerva*

The text of *Il gattopardo* has been the object of considerable debate. In preference to G. Lanza Tomasi's 1969 edition (Feltrinelli, Milan) of the 1957 manuscript I have used the first published edition (Feltrinelli, Milan, 1958), prepared by G. Bassani. It is to this edition that my page references correspond.

Both the textual problem and the Lampedusa controversy are discussed in some general works on the author: Giancarlo Buzzi, *Invito alla lettura di Tomasi di Lampedusa* (Mursia, Milan, 1972);

Simonetta Salvestroni, *Lampedusa* ('Il Castoro', La Nuova Italia, Florence, 1973); G. P. Samonà, *Il 'Gattopardo' e i 'Racconti' di Lampedusa* (La Nuova Italia, Florence, 1974). See also David Nolan, 'Lampedusa's *The Leopard*', in *Studies*, Winter, 1966, pp. 403-414.

Lampedusa's 'Lezioni su Stendhal' appeared in *Paragone* (1959), pp. 3-49. Louis Aragon's articles on Lampedusa are in *Lettres Françaises* of December 1959 and February 1960.

English translations: *The Leopard* (Collins and Harvill, London, 1960 and in the Fontana Library); *Two Stories and a Memory* (Collins and Harvill, London, 1962, and Penguin, Harmondsworth, 1966).

For an introduction to Italian thinkers whose outlook is strikingly consonant with Lampedusa's (or Fabrizio's?), see N. Bobbio, *Saggi sulla scienza politica in Italia* (Laterza, Bari, 1969), and H. S. Hughes, *Consciousness and Society* (MacGibbon and Kee, London, 1959 and Paladin, London, 1974).

*Ignazio Silone: the adventure of a poor socialist*

Silone's books are now all published by Mondadori, except *Uscita di sicurezza*, published by Vallecchi (Florence). Most of them exist in two, or even three, versions. My page references are to the definitive editions. An exhaustive bibliography and a comparative study of Silone's variants and revisions are to be found in Luce D'Eramo's indispensable *L'opera di Ignazio Silone* (Mondadori, Milan, 1971).

Some other useful works on Silone are: F. Virdia, *Silone* ('Il Castoro', La Nuova Italia, Florence, 1967); Jürgen Rühle, *Literature and Revolution* (first published in German in 1960; English translation by Jean Steinberg, Pall Mall Press, London, 1969: see 'Italy Between Black and Red', pp. 365-71, on Silone); Irving Howe, 'Ignazio Silone: Politics and the Novel' (reprinted from *Politics and the Novel*, Horizon Press, New York, 1957), in *From 'Verismo' to Experimentalism: Essays on the Modern Italian Novel*, cit. (see pp. 120-34); R. W. B. Lewis, 'Ignazio Silone: the Politics of Charity', in *The Picaresque Saint* (Gollancz, London, 1960), pp. 109-78; Jean Whyte, 'The Evolution of Silone's Central Theme', in *Italian Studies*, Vol. XXV, 1970, pp. 49-62.

Jonathan Cape, London, have published, in English translation, *The Seed beneath the Snow* (1943), *And He did Hide Himself* (1946), *A Handful of Blackberries* (1954, and Consul Books, London, 1962), *The School for Dictators* (1939; also published in another translation by

Gollancz, London, 1964), *The Secret of Luca* (1959) and *The Fox and the Camellias* (1961).

Gollancz, London, have published *Bread and Wine* (1964; Panther, London, 1967), which had appeared in an earlier version (Methuen, London, 1936); *Emergency Exit* (1969); and *The Story of a Humble Christian* (1970). *Fontamara* first appeared in English in 1934 (Methuen, London), then in several editions by Jonathan Cape, London, and in a paperback edition by Panther, London, 1967.

*Guareschi's microcosm: politics as play*
Guareschi's books are published by Rizzoli, Milan. Mina J. Moore Rinvolucri, 'The Creator of Don Camillo: Giovanni Guareschi', in *Modern Languages* (Journal of the Modern Languages Association), XXXIX, 3 (September, 1958), pp. 95-8, was the only study on Guareschi that went beyond the scope of a book review until the appearance, in 1977, after I had written this present piece, of G. F. Vene, *Don Camillo, Peppone, e il compromesso storico* (Sugar, Milan).

The 'Don Camillo' series, and other books by Guareschi, have been published in English translation by Gollancz, London, and also by Penguin, Harmondsworth.

*Cesare Pavese: from literature to suicide*
Pavese's works are published by Einaudi, Turin. His novels have been collected in *Romanzi*, two vols, (1961). See also: *Racconti* (1960); *Poesie edite e inedite* (1962); *Lettere*, two vols. (1966); *La Letteratura americana e altri saggi* (1951) contains frequent statements of his limited conception of political commitment in literature.

D. Lajolo's biography, *Il 'vizio assurdo'* (Il Saggiatore, Milan, 1960, and Gli Oscar, Mondadori, Milan, 1972), is attentive to Pavese's politics. D. Fernandez, *L'échec de Pavese* (Grasset, Paris, 1968), analyses his personality. The many critical studies include: A. Guiducci, *Il mito Pavese* (Vallecchi, Florence, 1967); G. Venturi, *Pavese* ('Il Castoro', La Nuova Italia, Florence, 1969); D. Heiney, 'Pavese', in *Three Italian Novelists* (University of Michigan Press, Ann Arbor, 1968), pp. 83-146; G. P. Biasin, *The Smile of the Gods* (Cornell University Press, 1969); V. Stella, *L'elegia tragica di Cesare Pavese* (Longo, Ravenna, 1969); P. Renard, *Pavese prison de l'imaginaire lieu d'écriture* (Larousse, Paris, 1972); E. Catalano, *Cesare Pavese fra politica e ideologia* (De Donato, Bari, 1976). The journal *Sigma* devoted nos 3-4 (1964) to Pavese.

Most of Pavese's writings have been published in English translation. See particularly *The Political Prisoner* (*Il carcere*; Peter Owen, London, 1955, and Mayflower paperback edition, London, 1966); *The Comrade* (Peter Owen, London, 1959); *The Moon and the Bonfire* (John Lehmann, London, 1952, and Penguin, Harmondsworth, 1963); *This Business of Living*, Pavese's diary (Peter Owen, London, 1961, and Consul Books, World Distributors, London, 1964) and *The House on the Hill* (Peter Owen, London, 1956, and Digit Books, Brown and Watson, London, 1963).

*Pier Paolo Pasolini: after Eros*
All Pasolini's books are published by Garzanti, Milan, unless otherwise stated.

   On Pasolini, see: G. C. Ferretti, 'La contrastata rivolta di P.', in *Letteratura e ideologia* (2nd ed., Editori Riuniti, Rome, 1964) and *Pasolini: l'universo orrendo* (Editori Riuniti, Rome, 1976); A. Asor Rosa, 'P', in *Scrittori e popolo* (*cit.*); T. Anzoino, *P.* ('Il Castoro', La Nuova Italia, Florence, 1971); O. Stack, *P. on P.: Interviews with Oswald Stack* (Thames and Hudson, London, 1969); T. O'Neill, 'A Problem of Character Development in P's Trilogy', in *Forum for Modern Language Studies*, Vol. V, 1969, pp. 80-4; *idem*, 'Il filologo come politico', in *Italian Studies*, Vol. XXV, 1970, pp. 63-78; and *idem*, 'Passione e ideologia', in *Forum for Modern Language Studies*, Vol. IX, 1973, pp. 346-62.

   In English there is *A violent life* (Jonathan Cape, London, 1968, and Panther, London, 1973).

*Calvino's macrocosm: the politics of play*
Calvino's narrative works are published by Einaudi.

   The most useful studies on Calvino are: Germana Pescio Bottino, *Calvino* ('Il Castoro', La Nuova Italia, Florence, 1967); J. R. Woodhouse, *Italo Calvino: A Reappraisal and an Appreciation of the Trilogy* (Hull University Press, 1968); *idem*, 'Italo Calvino and the Rediscovery of a Genre', in *Italian Quarterly*, XII, 45, 1968; *idem*, 'Fantasy, Alienation and the *Racconti* of Italo Calvino', in *Forum for Modern Language Studies*, VI, 4, 1970; *idem* (ed.), *Il barone rampante* (Manchester University, Press, 1970; with an introduction, bibliography, vocabulary and notes); Mario Boselli, '*Ti con zero* o la precarietà del progetto', in *Nuova Corrente*, 49, 1969; Giuseppe Bonura, *Invito alla lettura di Calvino* (Mursia, Milan, 1972); Antonio Illiano, 'Per una definizione della vena cosmogonica di Calvino: appunti su *Le cos-*

*micomiche* e *Ti con zero*', in *Italica*, 49, 3, 1972; Contardo Calligaris, *Italo Calvino* (Mursia, Milan, 1975).

For a fuller discussion of Calvino along the lines projected in this section, see my 'Calvino Ludens: Literary Play and its Political Implications', in *Journal of European Studies*, 5, 1975.

English translations of Calvino's works include: *The Path to the Nest of Spiders* (Collins, London, 1956); *The Baron in the Trees* (Collins, 1959); *The Non-Existent Knight* and *The Cloven Viscount* (Collins, 1962); *Cosmicomics* (Cape, London, 1969); *Time and the Hunter* (Cape, 1970); *Invisible Cities* (Secker and Warburg, London, 1975).

## *Terruggi's monster*

I have been unable to find any review or critical article on *Luisa e il presidente*. The journal Modern Fiction Studies, Vol. 23 No. 2 (Summer 1977), pp. 167-77, carries a brief introduction, 'An Unread Novel: Ugo Terruggi's *Luisa e il presidente*', with English translation of two chapters from the novel, by the present author.